Praise for *W.G.*

"Sibling authors Donna and William Burtch have unearthed a gem of a family story—and now bring it to the broader audience it richly deserves."

—**Michael Punke**, bestselling author of
The Revenant and *Ridgeline*

"A riveting account of a Baptist chaplain who stepped up as the first leader of Black troops to defend the Union cause during the Civil War, only to have that role erased by the War Department. This compelling work by Donna and William Burtch is certain to cause a reevaluation of a lost piece of U.S. history."

—**Ken Gormley**, *NYT* bestselling author and
President of Duquesne University

"A thorough and engaging bio of an obscure but pivotal player in some of the most important events in America's nineteenth century. From itinerant ministry, to enforcing martial law, raising the 1st U.S. Colored Troops [U.S.C.T.] in the Civil War, battling addiction, and faith healing, W. G. Raymond's story is a vividly rendered window into an era when men and women deeply believed, and acted boldly on their faith."

—**David Poyer**, *USA Today* bestselling author of
Thunder on the Mountain and *Heroes of Annapolis*

"A remarkable narrative about historical figure W. G. Raymond with themes of bravery and sacrifice from start to finish. A complex and flawed man, W.G. showed valor in the face of adversity as he derived strength from his belief in someth
The authors explore his unwavering convi

which can still be felt centuries later. This biography boldly declares that service matters yesterday, today, and forever."

—**Candace Brady**, VP of Advancement, National Veterans Memorial and Museum

"When William Gould Raymond published his now largely unknown autobiography in 1891, he used the title "Elder" and proclaimed that he shared his story in "the honor and glory of God." He also placed his descendants at the beginning of his list of those to whom he dedicated his volume. It is therefore no surprise that his account of his life focuses on his devotion to the human family. Yet as Donna Burtch and William Burtch have demonstrated in their updated version of their great-great-great grandfather's memoirs, Raymond did so much more. Through their research they provide additional evidence that not only corroborates but expands on Raymond's recollections and transcriptions of his personal and professional papers. During the mid-nineteenth century, Raymond preached for the Baptist Church, he was a key figure in the formation of the 1st United States Colored Infantry in the District of Columbia, and he assisted the Pottawatomie in Kansas. Later in the century he continued to serve the Baptist Church through his work as a faith healer and struggled with his own opium addiction. Raymond's experiences not only span the nineteenth century, but his journeys took him from New England to the upper South, and from the Native American reservations in Kansas to New York. General audiences will be fascinated by William Gould Raymond's personal story, but they will also benefit from the multiple lessons in United States history that are much needed for us to better understand our nation and citizenry today."

—**Kelly Mezurek**, author of *For Their Own Cause: The 27th United States Colored Troops*

W.G.

The Opium-addicted Pistol Toting Preacher
Who Raised the First
Federal African American Union Troops

DONNA BURTCH &
WILLIAM BURTCH

Mechanicsburg, PA USA

Published by Sunbury Press, Inc.
Mechanicsburg, Pennsylvania

SUNBURY
PRESS

www.sunburypress.com

For information about special discounts for bulk purchases, please contact Sunbury Press Orders Dept. at (855) 338-8359 or orders@sunburypress.com.

To request one of our authors for speaking engagements or book signings, please contact Sunbury Press Publicity Dept. at publicity@sunburypress.com.

FIRST SUNBURY PRESS EDITION: May 2022

Set in Adobe Garamond | Interior design by Crystal Devine | Cover by Danna Mathias Steele (Dearly Creative) | Edited by Lawrence Knorr.

Publisher's Cataloging-in-Publication Data
Names: Burtch Donna, author | Burtch, William, author.
Title: W.G. : the opium-addicted pistol toting preacher who raised the first Federal African American Union troops / Donna Burtch William Burtch.
Description: First trade paperback edition. | Mechanicsburg, PA : Sunbury Press, 2022.
Summary: Why were the first federal African American Union Army recruiting efforts in D.C. wiped from military records? Abraham Lincoln authorized W.G. Raymond to raise these courageous units. Addiction, family tragedy, thoughts of suicide and doubting his faith would dog W.G. He returned to D.C., where he had once been a star. Would he claw back?
Identifiers: ISBN 978-1-62006-908-0 (softcover).
Subjects: BIOGRAPHY & AUTOBIOGRAPHY / Historical | HISTORY / United States / Civil War Period (1850-1877) | HISTORY / United States / 19th Century.

Product of the United States of America
0 1 1 2 3 5 8 13 21 34 55

Continue the Enlightenment!

For Kari, with eternal love and gratitude.

—W.B.

For my family: past, present, future.

—D.B.

Contents

Preface

Why should a couple of reasonably contented Boomers consciously step away from their placating paths and routines to hibernate, to immerse themselves into the deepest crevices of obscure occurrences in the mid-19th century? Gather and sort through archived news clippings, torn pages in files at the Library of Congress, glean websites of historical societies and Civil War repositories? Delve into the life of a unique yet seldom contemplated man, William Gould (W.G.) Raymond? Why would we have undertaken this task?

The scourge of the COVID pandemic, and all of its implications, played a role. It took many of the usual pleasures and occupiers of our time off the table. Idle hours at home became the collective reality. One of us (William) had just lost his wife, Kari, to ovarian cancer, after a three-and-a-half-year journey of courage, inspiring peaks, and heartbreaking moments of crippling devastation; an inseparable couple for twenty-five years.

The imposed stillness of this period led our minds to crawl around behind the scenes. To stir up the nagging unfinished business, unanswered questions, the unsettled debates of life. Even the tedium of diligent research seemed attractive in such a situation. Writing a book assumed a plausibility that may not have emerged in ordinary times. And if that book addressed something of import to the greater awareness, all the better. That's the way we, as co-authors, felt about this project. A bit of the right time and the right topic coming together.

W.G. Raymond passed away in the late 19th century, and with him, an incredible, if at times seemingly inconceivable, story was buried. Within our family (we are siblings), the tale of W.G. was always floating around. Details were scant. Elders asserted that a photocopied version of W.G.'s autobiography was tucked away somewhere in one of our attics. More decades would pass.

At last, our Aunt Gayle, our mother's sister, stumbled across the loose leafed copy of W.G.'s book, held together by rubber bands. We passed it around. To a person, we were mesmerized by his story. One of faith, addiction, selfless national service, and a large and fluid Raymond family. A man who took risks in arenas most can only imagine.

William Gould Raymond was our great-great-great-grandfather.

In W.G.'s writings, details of a version of history that seemed largely untold, a recounting of events that involved none other than Abraham Lincoln and the recruitment of African American troops to serve in the first federal Black regiment in the District of Columbia. W.G.'s version appeared to differ in some material ways from standard historical treatments on the topic. The contrasts were not conflicting so much as the mainstream accounts of events seemed to omit elements that W.G. eloquently provided uniformly. Even the official government records seemed to be guilty of the same omissions.

We had to uncover the full truth.

Perhaps the most gratifying outcome of the research effort we poured into this project was that virtually all of W.G.'s assertions in his painstakingly meticulous autobiography were corroborated by press accounts, abridged and truncated mentions in other historical accounts, Abraham Lincoln's official library, unearthed correspondences of Senators and citizens, and the U.S. Government's own diverse departmental level websites. The story W.G. told was real. It was profound. And it was so little told.

At times it seemed as though we were led by a force we did not understand to impossibly arcane sources that filled some critical piece of the story puzzle. To cover our bases, we send a nod and a thank you to W.G.

Your story is at last out there where it belongs; may you rest in peace.

CHAPTER ONE

A Man and His Times

I t would be reasonable to conclude that a tale of war, the fight for the civil rights of the oppressed, spirituality, faith-healing, and altered consciousness through the abuse of drugs would pertain to the notorious 1960s. This, however, is a story of the 1860s and the decades immediately before and after.

The United States in the mid-1800s was a cauldron of conflict and promise: a land striving to define what it would become. The bloody Civil War raged. A ruminating and complex President was in the White House, possessing the power and heart to shape destiny.

At the core of the conflict for the country's future was slavery. While drawn in the geographic terms of North and South, the battle was a war waged within the souls and collective conscience of the people. At the tip of the spear was the District of Columbia, right in the middle of it all by its geography. And it housed the concentration of power.

William Gould Raymond, "W.G.," was as conflicted and complicated as the times. He was a man of modest means who often positioned himself at the center of momentous events. Events that shaped the tenor and path of America and civil rights. Despite his contributions, W.G. lived out his days in relative obscurity.

As remarkable as he was flawed, W.G.'s life was a mosaic of faith and his questioning of it, opium addiction, health setbacks, a sprawling family—some he recognized as such, some he did not—service as a

Union Army soldier and officer, then as a Lincoln-appointed hospital chaplain, horse breeder, and faith healer.

However, W.G.'s place in history would be staked as an initial commanding officer responsible for raising what became the 1st United States Colored Troops (U.S.C.T.) of the District of Columbia. This initiative was directly authorized by President Abraham Lincoln immediately following the Emancipation Proclamation. The result was the establishment of the first federal, rather than state-authorized, regiments of African American Union soldiers.

W.G., along with Pennsylvanian J.D. Turner and the Reverend Henry McNeal Turner, an African American, fought to raise these early all Black troops against a backdrop of fierce resistance and the threat of death. The troops and companies they recruited would wage arguably the most successful battle by African American and freedmen soldiers in the Civil War.

How did the courageous actions of these pioneering Union officers, and hundreds of Black soldiers, many escaped slaves fighting for their very freedom, slip through historical narratives of those remarkable early weeks of May 1863? How could these fledgling companies of African American soldiers, and their White Lincoln-appointed officers, be omitted from official War Department records? The answers lie in a complex web of politics, egos, a frenetic pace of change in a young country, a government seeking to appear in control, and a press struggling to keep up with it all.

What internal forces conspired within W.G. to drive him to enlist as a Union infantryman as a forty-three-year-old preacher, risk his life and scores of freedmen to raise a regiment of Black soldiers to fight slavery and the Confederacy? Where did he harvest the resolve to endure monumental challenges to his faith, his health, battle through addictions, the deaths of children and wives, and a marriage that dissolved into obscurity?

We will see that W.G. was a man who knew and owned his limitations and faults and found ways through or around them. Always there was a calling that he was driven to heed. A voice that he heard.

To have any hope of understanding W.G. and the gravity of his contribution to the country, it is necessary to understand from where he came; to know his very beginnings.

William Gould (W.G.) Raymond

CHAPTER TWO

The Birth and Spiritual Awakening of W.G. Raymond

William Gould Raymond was born into a New York farm family on Independence Day, 1819. His birth-place, Milo, New York, is nestled between two Finger Lakes, Keuka and Seneca. Not long after his birth, his family moved to the foot of Seneca Lake, three miles north of Geneva. In this lake, his self-professed connection to Satan was washed into oblivion.

His parents were devout members of the Baptist Church. His father was John Raymond (1791–1861), whose family traced back to England before establishing a presence in Connecticut and eventually claiming a foothold in New York. His mother was Julia Gould Raymond (1795–1885) of New York heritage.

As a young man, Willie and his good friend Ed Wayburn appreciated "earthly pleasures," and Willie had drifted away from "the religious counsels" of his parents. One night, he heard his mother's cries of anguish, "William is lost! William is lost!" She sobbed as her husband listened. Still, Will clung to the ways of the world.[1]

Eventually, he agreed to attend a revival meeting with his friend, but only to act "as spies" to mock the event later with their friends.

The revival made him nervous, and he said he felt the presence of the devil wrestling for his soul. His restlessness increased as he saw his father and his older brother David in a flood of tears begging him to go forward to be saved. He felt more resolved to resist the goal of the revival.

Finally, even Ed Wayburn said, "Will, let's go. I'll go if you will." He was furious with Ed and wanted to knock him from his seat. He could feel the power of his guiding force, the Devil, and he refused to bend down in prayer. Through the sweat forming on his brow, he could see those in attendance viewing him from their kneeled positions, making him a target of their prayers.

W.G. felt shame rising in his heart. He heard a voice say, "You are in danger." He could feel himself sliding into hell and cried tears yielding up the world as he said, "Farewell, vain world."[2]

The burden lifted from his soul. He felt a release. W.G. flung his arms around his father's neck and asked for forgiveness. He was lifted from despair and then immersed in Seneca Lake. This turbulent homecoming to his Baptist roots began the first step in his protracted and often dangerous service to the Lord.

W.G.'S EARLY PREACHING, COLLEGE, TRAVELS, AND TRAVAILS

W.G. was a ready preacher. After his conversion and following his baptismal immersion in Seneca Lake, he took to the streets holding meetings and "leading souls to Christ."

He journeyed with his mentor, Brother Jacob Knapp, in nearby Seneca Falls, New York. Following a second night of preaching in a private home, he went, close to midnight, to a church he found unlocked. Once inside, he and a man named Crittenden fell into deep prayer for hours. "Let's pray that God will send the people into the church and so disturb the people in the city that they cannot rest and give a new impetus to the meeting." People began to come in and out of the church despite the late hour, maybe drawn by the light.

W.G. said he lost full awareness of them—he could not break his intercession with God. He felt as though he would end the night, leaving his body and going "with God."[3]

Then for a moment, he "entered Paradise" and saw several visions, some of which he chose never to reveal. What he did say of the moment was startling: "I saw a literal lake of fire and brimstone and thousands of people passing down an inclined plane and falling into a bottomless pit."[4]

With little sleep, W.G. journeyed with Brother Knapp to Elmira, New York, and Rochester. He gained confidence watching Brother Knapp facing the "rage of Satan;" in particular, he noted that the gamblers at the Monroe House opposed their revival work.

While prayers were earnestly voiced in the church, these gamblers held court every night in the nearby Monroe House. Brother Knapp publicly exposed this in the church. This led one of the gamblers to rise up, shouting, "You are a liar!" A deacon moved to have him arrested. Brother Knapp urged that the deacon leave him alone.

The following night people gathered around the church and in the street. As many as a thousand desperate characters gathered, some wielding pistols.

Brother Knapp raised his hand and intoned in a booming voice, "Be seated. It is a false alarm, a trick of the devil. I have a sermon to preach, and I shall preach it unless I am shot down."

Detractors hurled stones through the church windows. Brother Knapp raised his hand and said, "They do not want to hurt you but to kill me. Kneel down."

All knelt.[5]

At that moment, a flash of lightning caused the lights in the church to dim. Another volley of stones came, followed by a clap of thunder that shook structures. Still another volley of stones came. Then, following another blast of thunder and strike of lightning, the stones ceased. The crowd wandered away and dispersed. W.G. said of the night, "The wicked flee when no man pursueth, but the righteous are as bold as a lion."[6]

While in Rochester, W.G. preached his first sermon at the request of Deacon Sage. His "healing power" was also first exhibited in these early days in Rochester. "I was asked to visit a lady whose name I have forgotten, that was suffering from nervous prostration and the last stages of consumption and was unsaved. I prayed not only for her salvation but recovery, and she was immediately raised up and saved."

Soon W.G. returned home to labor on the family farm. He was called upon to chop wood. His father, John, soon noticed the lackluster effort he brought to the ax. It was as if he paused on each back motion, suspended in thought. His father shared this observation with W.G.'s mother.

The following day a church member named Hadley came to the house and said, "William, the Lord has called you to preach the gospel. We are going to send you to Hamilton."

W.G. attended Hamilton Literary and Theological Institution (now Colgate University). It did not take long before the president of the College, the Reverend Dr. Nathaniel Kendrick, took notice of him.[7]

W.G.'s passion for preaching and reaching out to save souls kept him restless. He lived with his mentor, Jacob Knapp, and his family to keep his expenses in check. This gave him the opportunity he craved to listen to stories of Knapp's ongoing evangelistic work. W.G. listened for hours to Knapp's accounts of deliverances from enemies and conversion and was instructed by Knapp's preaching of the Gospel.

W.G., the student, began to hold meetings in some of the schoolhouses around the villages. One night, he chose to preach the text, "No Hope." He was stunned to find that fifteen people came forward from among the most "wicked" to be saved.

"One old man by the name of Morse, nearly eighty years old, rose up and said, 'Young man, I have been blind twenty years; I have been a Universalist for much longer than that. Until now, I had a hope, but you have destroyed it. What shall I do to be saved? I feel I am a lost soul.'"[8]

W.G. and his followers gathered around Morse and prayed for his soul. Time passed. Finally, the old man rose, rejoicing, exclaiming that he was a new man.

When Morse died, he left a small amount for W.G. to continue his studies.[9]

He still struggled with his lack of means. But he was encouraged to persevere because of the grace of a child: the old man's granddaughter, Mary Morse, eight years old, gave him clear evidence of her own conversion. She and her little sisters prayed three times a day. Unfortunately, little Mary fell ill. She clung to her faith and said, "I am going where Jesus is, and I want you to pray just as I have prayed," she said to her mother and little sisters. Then she called to her father, who was a "wicked" man. She said, "Pa, I am going to die and go where Jesus is. Pa, I want you to make me a promise that you won't swear anymore and that you won't take God's name in vain anymore." The man made the promise to his dying child.

Moments later, she passed away, saying, "Pa, do you see those angels coming . . . Do you see them, Pa?"[10]

When the news of her passing reached W.G., and he paid a second visit to the family, he said, "Lord, I will preach the Gospel if I can only lead a child to Christ." Ever after, he thought of Mary Morse as his guardian angel.[11]

W.G.'s commitment to his studies began to wane. He lost confidence in some of the faculty, most notably President Kendrick. W.G. encouraged another student, John Tallman, to request leave with him to go out and labor to "procure means to help us through the coming year." They sought permission from Professor George W. Eaton, professor of Church and Ecclesiastical History. They planned to go to New York City, where Brother Knapp held meetings.

They started out with a dollar and a half in their pockets, intending to walk hundreds of miles to Albany, Cooperstown, and New York City. Tallman's feet gave out after several days of hiking through the muddy roads of early spring.

Finding them nearly starving, one hostess at a Baptist Tavern gave them ham and eggs. When the stagecoach arrived, they showed the driver they only had half the fare. W.G. said, "'Friend, this is all we've got, and Tallman's feet won't let him walk any further.' He was impressed that we had walked all the way from Hamilton College and said, 'Young men get in and ride with me to Albany.'"[12]

A man by the name of Brother Illsby, the pastor of First Baptist Church, Brooklyn, asked Brother Knapp to secure a student to visit his church and hold meetings. W.G. was recommended and soon began to visit members of the congregation. At night, he would sing "Old Ship Zion." The church leaders presented him with a broadcloth suit when he left.[13]

Next, he was called to officiate in Dr. Cone's Church, the First Baptist Church of New York City. He also preached on board vessels in the East River, where over a thousand would come and listen to his prayers and his singing of "Old Ship Zion." He was also popular as a Sunday School speaker.

Dr. Spencer Houghton Cone had attended Princeton University at just twelve years old, abandoning his studies when his father became ill. Later, during the War of 1812, he was at the Battle of Bladensburg and wrote an account of this experience in "Some Account of the Life of Spencer Houghton Cone, A Baptist Preacher in America." Cone was converted to the Baptist Church in 1814. In 1815–16 he became Chaplain of the United States House of Representatives.[14]

All was coming together for W.G. until Dr. Kendrick came to New York City. W.G.'s name was frequently mentioned, and learning that it was indeed his student who was gaining the attention, Dr. Kendrick said, "Why he is but a young student and left the institution without permission."[15]

Crestfallen, W.G. returned to Hamilton. Kendrick himself addressed W.G., "How was it that you left the college without permission?" W.G. replied firmly that he and John Tallman had the permission of Professor George Eaton. Dr. Kendrick replied, "I doubt it."[16]

The two students were called before the faculty. In front of the professors, Dr. Kendrick said, "We admire your zeal and believe you to be devoted Christians, and we all want to save your reputation. Dr. Eaton apparently gave you permission to leave but not to go to New York City. That is where we send advanced students." Dr. Kendrick asked that W.G. and Tallman make a confession and an apology.[17]

This angered W.G. He said, "Gentlemen of the faculty, I never shall do it, and you can expel me at your pleasure. If the Lord has called me to preach the Gospel, he will open some way for my education so that it will not be necessitated to confess to a lie."

President Kendrick said in front of all, "You have too much zeal, and you find when you get into work, you will want more knowledge and less zeal." In the end, W.G. was required to confess or be suspended.

Tallman made his confession. W.G. remained resolute. He was suspended. The school sent a faculty member to Brother Knapp's, requesting that he help to bring W.G. to confession. Brother Knapp said, "No, I will not. God will open a way for his education."[18]

Hamilton, New York campus in the 1800s (*Harper's Weekly*, April 23, 1892).

Kendrick then sent W.G.'s beloved mathematics teacher, Professor Stephen W. Taylor. He said, "Brother Raymond, I do not believe that the faculty understand you. You know now what the college rules are. Would you leave the college now without telling us where you are going?"

"No," W.G. said, "I would not, though I regard the requirements as tyrannical . . . I am a law-abiding man."

The next day, W.G. was restored to his class, though it still riled W.G. that Dr. Kendrick had never recanted the statement he'd made in New York that W.G. and John Tallman had left without permission.[19]

By then, far behind in his studies, W.G. decided to leave Knapp's home and live in a boarding house. This meant he had to walk further to and from school, and with a change of diet, hard study, anxiety, and confinement to his room, he became exhausted and ill.

He suffered from deep stomach pains and began, on horseback, a journey home that took several months. He preached all along the way.[20]

"I spent several months in the vicinity of the Allegheny mountains, and from there to Canada and Niagara Falls, preaching to the Scotch Highlanders among whom souls were gloriously saved and returned home much improved in health, though not rid of dyspepsia."

During the decade or so that followed his return to his family home, and as his general health improved, W.G. deepened his avocation into his vocation, becoming an ordained Baptist minister on February 27, 1843.[21]

He accepted assignments and calls in New York mission fields. These smaller churches were not locally self-supporting and depended partly on support from the larger Baptist organization. He moved among the churches in Wheeler, Avoca, Howard Flats, Towlesville, Livingston, and Jasper, New York, and was also afforded less income than the more established churches could provide. He supplemented his income by working the land upon which he and his family lived.

CHAPTER THREE

Enlistment in the 86th
New York Infantry

W.G.'s stance on slavery, and thus the Civil War, came to be revealed through his words and sermons.

During a sermon to his congregation on a Sunday in early 1861, in passionate support of the Union Civil War effort, W.G. preached, ". . . cursed be he that keepeth back his sword from blood," quoting from *Jeremiah* 48:10.[1]

W.G. was most demonstrative of his abolitionist stance through his actions. He strongly encouraged citizens of his county and eligible members of his congregation to enlist, fight for the cause of the Union Army, and end slavery.

He recalled of that afternoon that after the service, a wealthy local man, a church member, challenged him, asking why he did not enlist, the insinuation being that W.G. was all words and no action—perhaps he was even a coward.

W.G. had to that point posited that being a man of the cloth, a forty-three-year-old father and husband, and by his own description corpulent, he was not a candidate for battle.

However, after prayerful reflection, he informed his wife that he had changed his mind. "I am going to the War," he announced, to which she laughed. Nevertheless, the following morning he mounted his Black Hawk Morgan horse and located General Robert B. Van Volkenburgh,

86th New York Infantry Officers

who gave him authority to raise a company. Raymond and his company were mustered into service in Elmira, New York, where W.G. became 1st Lieutenant of Company H in the 86th New York Infantry, also known as the Steuben Rangers. The 86th engaged in several battles and lost over three hundred men before being mustered out of service in 1865.

During this period, signs of W.G.'s budding compassion for the plight of African Americans were revealed again during his time as a Steuben Ranger. Two instances, one involving an older Black woman and the other a young Black lad, were telling.

In October of 1861, W.G. was ordered to the front. While in a camp in Maryland to assist in constructing a fort, W.G. went hunting with fellow soldiers. They came upon a small shack sheltering an old Black woman, who invited them in.

W.G. told the woman she appeared ill and asked about her health and background.

"Yes honey, I'se very poorly," she told them. "I expect I'm a hundred and seven."[2]

She spoke of her origins and her master in the South. She had been a field hand and was mother to ten children, of which a few were born ". . . right in the field as I was at work."

Three of her children, sons, were fathered by her master. She related that each was sold for two thousand dollars.[3]

". . . you don't say your master sold his own sons?" W.G. asked.

"[Lord] yes, that's nothin'," the old woman replied, explaining that she couldn't stop her master from selling their sons. W.G. and the soldiers then prayed with her.

So moved were they by this woman and her circumstances, W.G. and the soldiers kept her in firewood and food until her death.[4]

W.G. sent word to her master, informing him of her passing. He asked if he planned to bury her.

". . . I'll have nothing to do with her," was the prompt and curt reply.

W.G. and fellow soldiers then crafted a wooden coffin and conducted a proper and respectful burial for her.[5]

While still in Maryland, the next incident involved a small Black youth known as Clem, who had been an assistant to W.G. One day, soldiers informed W.G. that Clem had been captured.

After tracking him down in a blacksmith's shop, W.G. asked Clem to point out the man who had detained him.

Clem pointed to the blacksmith.

1st Lieut. W.G. Raymond, 86th New York Infantry (Official Portrait)

"Clem," W.G. explained to the blacksmith, ". . . is on the payroll" and worked for him.

The blacksmith had designs on turning Clem over for the twenty-five-dollar reward paid for runaway slaves. W.G. rescued the boy after threatening a price to be paid, both physically and monetarily, by the blacksmith.[6]

Upon W.G. and Clem's return to the regiment, the unit shouted, "Three cheers for Clem!" Joyous songs and "patting juba" followed. Soon after, when W.G. took ill, he credited Clem with saving his life through his devoted care.[7]

CHAPTER FOUR

War Detective Appointment and Incidents of 1863

Around that time, W.G. and his unit were ordered to Washington, D.C. Once there, W.G. was assigned command of the Provost Guard, receiving a post under General Lafayette C. Baker, Colonel and Provost Marshal. Among his orders from the War Department were to contain the rampant gambling and liquor operations threatening to consume the district.

As Provost Guard Detective, W.G. shut down bars in the renowned Willard Hotel and Hammack's restaurant, disrupting access to liquor for various ranking government officials. Establishments that harbored prostitution, such as the Iron Clad House, were also in his sights. He locked down high-stakes gambling operations, prompting offers of bribes which reportedly reached an astounding forty thousand dollars.[1]

"No! Money can't buy me," he'd snap, content with his government salary and keeping his integrity intact.[2]

W.G. continued to encounter an assortment of conflicts needing his official engagement. One evening he was drawn to the cries of an African American woman from a rooftop. Men by the names of Allen, Wise, and Berry had the rest of the woman's family in a cage already.[3] Berry claimed to be the master of the captives. W.G. intervened and demanded evidence to support their assertions. Ultimately, he arrested Allen and Wise for kidnapping,[4] and they were bound over to the Old Capitol Prison.[5]

When Allen was released from prison, W.G. met him by chance on the street. They stopped and faced each other.

"Damn you," Allen cursed.

". . . it's a good time to settle it now," W.G. said.

Allen saw the pistol in W.G.'s hand and passed on.[6]

In her Pulitzer Prize-winning account of 1860 to 1865 Washington, Margaret Leech describes W.G. as ". . . fanatical in his devotion to his work." So diligent was his rousting of prostitutes and their johns, often soldiers and D.C. dignitaries, that they ". . . scurried before the tramp of [W.G.] Raymond's squad in the street below."[7]

W.G. then spent some time at Frederick City, Maryland, and discovered it was crawling with enemies of the government. For a week or ten days, W.G. moved between Point of Rocks, Berlin, and Harpers Ferry, and during this short time, confiscated nearly one hundred thousand dollars of property.[8]

"I ordered a notorious rebel, a blockade runner, into the same arsenal where John Brown defended himself. I visited Charlestown where John Brown, Cook, and others were executed," he recalled.

He then journeyed up the Shenandoah to an area perched between the North and the South to see a man he wanted to hire. W.G. was looking for his assistance in capturing John Mobberly (also known as Mobley or Morbly), a notorious guerrilla and thief.

"I rode up to the top of the mountain and had occasion to stop. I had a presentiment that Mobberly was coming, seeming to hear his horses, and the rattling of his sabers, but looking in the direction of the sounds, for miles, I could see nothing."

W.G. started down the mountain and led his horse to the river. He paused and again heard sounds of sabers rattling together.

"I hurried back to the point of observation but still could discover nothing."

W.G. felt unsettled, even nervous, to the point he gave up trying to find the man. He mounted his horse and tried to steady his nerves. It was the first time, while in service, he felt fearful.

In less than an hour, the news came to Harpers Ferry that Mobberly had indeed passed right down where he had been and captured three men of the family where W.G. was to have dined.[9]

THE PROVOST GUARD AND THE DRINKING-
HOUSES —*Editor Star*—Dear Sir: As an officer
of the Provost Guard in this city, permit me to
state for the public, through your columns, that I
have been pleased to find that nearly all the principal hotels in the city comply with the military
requ rements in regard to the sale of liquors; and
that while endeavoring to execute all ord·rs and
enforce the laws, I find it is the unlicensed shops
and low drinking saloons that are the principal
cause of so much disorder and ruffianism among
the soldiers.

We have found the law-abiding citizens sym-
pathizing with our efforts to preserve the good
order of the city, and have received the assistance of the city police whenever needed; for
which we desire to tender our sincere thanks.

It is my firm conviction that three-fourths of
the robberies committed upon our soldiers are
perpetrated by the inmates of these low places of
public resort, and a large share of them by per-
sons belonging to other localities, who are making
a temporary stay here for the sole purpose of plun-
dering soldiers. Many of them wear portions of
U. S. uniforms to aid them in their infamous designs upon the soldiers.

We learn by the statements of some of the soldiers that two or three drinks of ale make them
perfectly senseless, or crazy, in a few minutes,
and thus they are easily robbed.

Let me say to the keepers of such shops, if they
continue to sell ale or other liquors to soldiers, or
keep their shops open later than 9½ o'clock in
the evening, they may expect the full penalty of
the law.

Let us have the good wishes and co-operation
of all lovers of peace and good order, in our
efforts to protect the city from the corrupting and
demoralizing influence of these violators of the
laws.

Grateful for the courtesy extended to us, in per-
mitting us to make such statements through your
columns as may from time to time be proper to
publish in relation to the Provost Guard,

I remain your humble servant,

W. G. RAYMOND,
1st Lieut. of City Patrol, 86th Reg't N. Y. Vol.
Washington, May 19, 1862.

W.G. Letter to Editor (*Evening Star,* May 20, 1862)

W.G. said, "Had it not been for the presentiment given me, (I believe, of the Lord), I should have been captured with the others, and no doubt hung right there, as I had my silver badge inside my vest."

W.G.'s detective days were often frightening. "I went down to Point of Rocks to watch the runaways of smugglers. The Provost Marshal had promised me men for that night to assist me. A young man being with me, we rode out to a farmhouse to feed the horses and get supper. I had neglected to get the countersign, as it did not occur to me that they had a guard. On my return, we tarried to water the horses at a brook. As we were riding up a little elevation, a gun was fired, the contents passing close by the young man. Then the command: 'Halt!' was given. Very quickly, thirteen soldiers with pointed guns were standing just front, within a few rods of us. The guns were cocked, ready to fire; if one had fired, all would have done so. This frightened our horses so that we couldn't come to a halt, and I said so, and still he cried, 'Halt!' I said, 'I have halted but can't keep the horse's feet still.'"

The sentinel who had fired had reloaded his gun and was just putting the cap on. W.G. shouted, "You holler halt to me again or move your gun, I'll shoot you dead; I am a friend without the countersign. Is the Lieutenant of Guard present?"

The sentinel remained silent. W.G. repeated the question. A soldier said, "Yes." Up to this time, the men had made no effort to learn the identities of W.G. and the young man.

W.G. said, "Lieutenant, come down here, and I will show you I am a man of authority." He started, then all at once made as if to go back. W.G. said, "If you go back, I'll shoot you dead." The man came up to W.G. trembling. "I said, in an undertone, 'put your hand on this badge,' and as he did so, I said, 'Detective of the War Department.'"

The Lieutenant shouted out, "All right, Guards to your post." W.G. went with them into headquarters. On the way, W.G. said, "You have been playing sharp tonight, and if I knew that you have given the order to shoot and then cried halt, I would shoot you down in your tracks this minute, for the captain knew that a Detective of the War Department would come through these lines tonight. We could have shot you all down in half a minute, as we are well-armed, and I thought you were Mobberly."

John W. Mobberly military portrait

Just months later, John Mobberly died at age twenty by the hand of a man he had tortured and left to die.[10] Ranger Charles Stewart had been shot execution-style. Mobberly and his horse rode over him, back and forth, taunted him, and laughed as he shot him. Then he took Stewart's boots from his crumpled body in a final act of depravity.[11]

He could not have known that the man who had been shot several times and trampled had survived. He had been carried to a nearby home and attended to by Dr. Thomas Bond, who said, "My only ambition in life is to live long enough to make another hell for the man that shot Stewart after he was helpless."

Mobberly and his gang had also taken a man named Law out and staked him so animals or exposure would kill him.[12] In a 1920 article in the *Confederate Veteran*, Magnus Thompson, a fellow member of the 35th Virginia Cavalry, stated that Mobberly had "killed more Yankees than any man in the Army of Northern Virginia . . . The devil could not catch him."

On April 5, 1865, Mobberly's time drew short. Ranger Charles Stewart, who had survived being shot and trampled, and a group of five other locals ambushed him at Luther H. Potterfield's barn near Lovettsville, Virginia.[13]

"Oh Lord, I am gone," he said before being shot by the six men who fired on him at close range.

At about this time, there was a growing belief among those in power in Washington and within the leadership of the Union Army that the wounded from battle mounting up in the nation's hospitals needed divine reinforcement for both physical and spiritual healing. President Lincoln, in response, appointed W.G. Raymond as Chaplain of the Hospitals at Washington, including the Trinity General Hospitals, in July of 1862.

W.G. applied the same enthusiasm in this new capacity as he had during his Provost Guard days. "The first abuse I sought to correct," he recalled, "was the manner in which they buried the soldiers, the imperfect coffins, full of cracks, the number they would dump into one wagon, putting them into graves half-filled with water and leaving them uncovered until the next day, or longer."

W.G. also headed off a plan to move dozens of severely wounded soldiers to a different location, which would have resulted in the deaths of many in transit.[14]

"I was soon in the presence of Senator Wilson of Massachusetts and his wife, who had done many acts of kindness to the afflicted soldiers and well knew their physical condition," W.G. told Senator Wilson that he wanted General Hammond's plan countermanded.

Senator Henry Wilson was a kindred spirit and was on the same side of the ledger on the big issues with W.G. In fact, he had been driven to enter politics because of his vehement opposition to slavery. "We must destroy slavery, or it will destroy liberty," he had declared to the Massachusetts legislature.[15] He was one W.G. knew he could count on to do the right thing in the right moment.

Senator Wilson could see the value in what W.G. was saying.

W.G. continued, "I want you to see Secretary Stanton in person tonight and tell him that not less than thirty or forty patients will die if removed."

Together they called on Senator Preston King of New York: "I asked him to write a letter to Secretary Stanton requesting him to countermand General Hammond's order and thereby save the lives of thirty or forty sick soldiers." Senator King quickly wrote the letter.[16]

"I started to see Brother Roberts, who lived near City Hall, believing he had personal influence with Stanton. We met him just starting for church and requested him to take this letter of King's at once to Stanton, and Senator Wilson would be there."

Roberts paused and said, "We have just started for church." His wife said, "Never mind the church. God will excuse us tonight." Mrs. Roberts had given more than one thousand dollars to help the soldiers in the hospitals. On a personal level, she knew what shape the afflicted soldiers were in and what the toll of moving the injured and ailing would be. Mr. Roberts went immediately to Secretary Stanton.

The order was countermanded the following day, a day of rejoicing.[17]

For his efforts, an impressive Bible was presented to W.G. with the following inscription: "Presented to W.G. Raymond, Chaplain Trinity General Hospital, by the Medical Officers, Attendants, and the Patients of the Hospital, as a tribute to his worth. Washington D.C., Feb. 1863."

W.G. was honorably discharged in April 1863.[18]

CHAPTER FIVE

Recruitment of the 1st U.S.C.T. of the District of Columbia, 1863

Foundational yet obscure back stories of the perilous moments and days immediately before and following President Lincoln's decision to allow African American Union Army regiments to fight in the Civil War exist. Too many have slipped through the public consciousness. The explosive and frenetic convergence of events unfolded faster than could be adequately recorded. W.G. Raymond's became one of so many pivotal stories largely disappearing into the mists of time. These omissions have been at the expense of the full comprehension of the arc of civil rights progress and the arc of the United States as a country.

Lincoln's historic Emancipation Proclamation in January 1863 set in motion a push for federally raised African American troops beyond the point of return. Though not directly authorized by Lincoln, state-level regiments of Black soldiers had already been raised and were fighting for their very freedom[1]—witness the story of the 54th Massachusetts Infantry Regiment and the historic gravity of its Black soldiers' blood sacrifice.

Lincoln struggled to settle on his view concerning Blacks fighting in the Union Army at either the state or federal level. Among the many things that concerned him was the potential, or the likelihood, for the mistreatment of captured Black troops.[2] *The New York Times*

President Abraham Lincoln

editorialized that caution was in order and that recruitment of African Americans could further widen the divide in the country.[3] Once the Emancipation Proclamation was pronounced the Law of the Land, however, it became difficult to assign logic to deny African Americans the right to fight for their freedom.[4]

Orator, writer, and statesman Frederick Douglass, a former slave, had the ear and, importantly, the respect of President Lincoln. He was an eloquent and fiery champion of equality for all races. Douglass fought tirelessly for the raising of federal Union regiments of Black soldiers and persistently kept the issue in front of Lincoln.

In time, Lincoln came to see the rightness and the necessity of Black Union soldiers. Ultimately, he asserted that the Civil War would not have been won without the bravery and sacrifice of the Black soldiers.

"Throw [the African American contribution] away, and the Union goes with it."[5]

Against this heady and swirling backdrop, individuals with various motives began to come to the fore in Washington, eager to take leadership roles in advancing African American engagement in the War. Some saw a quick path to achieving rank, command, and notoriety in the Union Army. Others were drawn to the risk, adventure, and the unknown. Regardless, all were certain to face challenges, resistance, and peril.

Two White chaplains, who had already served in the Union Army, heeded the call for the military leadership to advance federal African American regiments. The men were J.D. Turner of Pennsylvania, and W.G. Raymond.

W.G.'s proximity to Washington, his support for ending slavery, and his newfound time and energy complemented the swelling enthusiasm for African Americans to join the fight alongside White Union troops.

Frederick Douglass

W.G. Raymond professed and preached that slavery was wrong; freedom and liberty were meant for all. Most historic accounts reveal a consistency of viewpoint and actions relating to W.G. in this regard.

The Baptist Church may have helped to shape his positions. In the *Minutes of the Fifth Session of the Erie Baptist Association* held in the Baptist Church in the Village of Nashville, Chautauqua County, New York, on August 3, September 1 and 2, 1852, the Baptists made the following statement:

"Indeed, the Christian Church of the present day has entered upon a period in her history in which the precious word of God is being distributed as if borne on the wings of the four winds of heaven, both to the cottage of the peasant and the palace of the prince. The gates of the pagan nations are thrown open and invite the entrance of her missionaries to reap their ripened fields, while Africa's oppressed sons and daughters stretch forth their manacled hands in eloquent pleadings for liberty and the bread of life." In addition to W.G., many leaders of the Baptist Church were present during this session.[6]

In April of 1863, J.D. Turner and W.G. Raymond wrote persuasive letters to President Lincoln. Impressive recommendations from political leaders supported these letters. The two men requested authorization to move forward with the raising of African American troops for the District of Columbia, an infantry that would comprise the first federally raised Black troops in the Union Army.[7]

J.D. Turner wrote to Lincoln, "I have always, since my earliest recollection, sympathized with the oppressed . . . and labored for their elevation."[8]

In his letter to Lincoln, W.G. Raymond stated that he was ". . . anxious to put down this rebellion."[9] He was also quoted as saying that a federal regiment of African American soldiers from D.C. ". . . would go through the rebel states like electricity" and that Southern slaves would "rise *en masse* . . ."[10]

W.G. wrote a second letter to the President penned on the same day. He underscored his commitment by stating that he had a wife and four children. He told of his brief service as a commissioned officer and that he had served as a chaplain. His letter concluded: "I am nearly

Washington April 25 1865

His Excellency.
President Lincoln
Dear Sir.

I entered the service as a private, the 1st of Sept. 1861 with a number of men sufficient to compose a company. Within three days I was elected First Lieut. and continued in that position for eleven months. Four months of which, I was officer of the "Provost Guard" of this City, and my acts are publicly known

My connection with the 60th N.Y. Vol's. closed the 24th of last July, on accepting the commission of "Post Chaplain" from your Excellency and was assigned to the "Trinity General Hospital" at Washington

I served there faithfully & until "Honorably discharged" the thirteenth of this month

I refer you to Chaplain Smith and Dr. "Gurley's letter" for my faithfulness in that department—

I am here with my wife and four children and intended to make it my permanent residence, at least through this administration, as my whole soul and life is in it. But shall be compelled to leave unless assigned to duty

23154

Page 1 of W.G.'s letter to President Lincoln

elsewhere. I question whether you have a
more zealous supporter of your administration,
and, endorses your proclamations more heartily
than I do.

This letter will be handed to you by
"Commissioner Dole", who will inform you of
my experience and knowledge of the
white and "black" population of this District.
Accompanying this is my petition and references
asking the privilege of raising a "colored
Regiment" in this District and vicinity.
I believe the Rev. Mr. Turner and myself can
raise a "reg't" within sixty days. I have
many influential friends who have promised
to assist me. Many of the intelligent
colored men of this city have signed a
petition to that affect. I have been unanimously
endorsed by one of the "Union Leagues"
of which Com. Dole is President.

I write this letter of explanation so that
my petition may be short.

I am now nearly "Forty five" years of age
and have been a Baptist Clergyman for
twenty five years.

All of which I respectfully submit
for your decision.

Yours Truly

W. G. Raymond..
Ex. bishop.

Page 2 of W.G.'s letter to President Lincoln

Abraham Lincoln papers

From William G. Raymond to Abraham Lincoln, April 25, 1863

Washington April 25 1863

Dear Sir.

I entered the service as a private, the 7th of Sept. 1861. with a number of men sufficient to compose a company. Within three days I was elected First Lieut. and continued in that position for eleven months. Four months of which, I was officer of the "Provost Guard." of this City, and my acts are publicly known

My connexion with the 86th N. Y. Vols. closed the 24th of last July, on accepting the commision of "Post Chaplain" from your Excellency, and was assigned to the "Trinity General Hospital" at Washington

I served them faithfully [&] until "Honorably discharged" the thirteenth of this month I refer you to Chaplain Smith and Dr. "Gurley's letter" for my faithfulness in that department[1]

1 See Phineas D. Gurley to Lincoln, April 8, 1863.

I am here with my wife and four children and intended to make it my permanent residence, — at least through this Administration. As my whole soul and life is in it. But shall be compelled to leave unless assigned to duty elsewhere. I question whether you have a more zealous supporter of your Adminstration, and one who endorses your proclamations more heartily than I do.

This letter will be handed to you by "Commisioner Dole",[2] who will inform you of my experience and knowledge of the white and "black" population of this District Accompanying this is my petition and references asking the privilege of raising a "Colored Regiment" in this District and vicinity I believe the Rev. Mr. Turner and myself can raise a "Reg't" within sixty days. I have many influential friends who have promised to assist me. Many of the intelligent "colored men" of this city have signed a petition to that affect. I have been unanimously endorsed, by one of the "Union Leagues" of which Com. Dole is President

2 William P. Dole

I write this letter of explanation so that my petition may be short

Translation of W.G.'s Letter to President Lincoln page 1 (Abraham Lincoln Papers, Library of Congress)

LIBRARY OF CONGRESS

I am now nearly "Forty five" years of age and have been a Baptist Clergyman for Twenty five years

All of which I respectfully subm[it] for your decision[3]

---

3 Lincoln wrote a letter to Secretary Stanton and requested him to look into the matter. See *Collected Works*, VI, 212.

Yours Truly

W. G. Raymond,,

Ex. Chap

Trinity Hospital

Translation of W.G.'s Letter to President Lincoln page 2 (Abraham Lincoln Papers, Library of Congress)

Senator Preston King, New York   Senator Charles Sumner, Massachusetts

forty-five years of age and have been a Baptist clergyman for twenty-five years, all of which I respectfully submit for your decision."[11]

Former Senator from New York, Preston King, wrote to Secretary of War Edwin Stanton on W.G.'s behalf, stating that he was ". . . faithful and zealous . . . and devoted to the cause of the country."[12] Senator Charles Sumner of Massachusetts also strongly praised W.G.[13]

W.G. and Turner presented their plans to President Lincoln, accompanied by Commissioner William P. Dole (Indian Affairs), an advocate of the effort. Following that meeting, Lincoln ordered Secretary Stanton to do all in his power to assist them in raising the regiment.[14] Lincoln's memo of instruction to Stanton, and related notes, are cataloged in *The Collected Works of Abraham Lincoln, Volume VI* (The Abraham Lincoln Association). Turner and W.G. were named the initial commanding officers, colonel and lieutenant colonel, respectively.[15]

Commissioner Dole, W.G., and Turner next met with Secretary Stanton. At first, Stanton balked, throwing Lincoln's letter down.[16] (It is well documented that Stanton had a high sensitivity to interference from anyone, including Lincoln, to his War Department affairs.)

LOCAL AFFAIRS.

THE COLORED VOLUNTEERS.—By a notice in our special column to-day, it will be seen that the new regiment will assemble to-day for organization. We learn that Commissioner Dole, with Colonels Turner and Raymoud, and other friends of the movement, visited the President to-day, to present the rolls and tender the services of about 800 men already enlisted, and to ask for quarters, etc. They were gladly received, and the President at once referred them to the Secretary of War, with a request that he "do the very best for them he could." Secretary Stanton has given orders that when 640 men, who will pass inspection, are presented, they will be mustered in at once and assigned to quarters. It is certainly gratifying to record the success of this important movement. The whole country is looking on this regiment with interest. We believe that both officers and men will not disappoint the expectations of all true patriots.

A meeting will be held at six o'clock this afternoon on the green in rear of the Big Bethel church, South Capitol street.

Daily National Republican (Second Edition), May 12

REGIMENT OF NEGROES.—Public notice is given to the officers and men of the proposed Regiment of District of Columbia (colored) Volunteers to assemble to-morrow for the purpose of inspection and being mustered into service. The Republican says:—"Commissioner Dole, with Colonels Turner and Raymond, and other friends of the movement, visited the President to-day to present the rolls and tender the services of about 800 men already enlisted, and to ask for quarters, &c. They were gladly received, and the President at once referred them to the Secretary of War, with a request that he would "do the very best for them he could." Secretary Stanton has given orders that when 640 who will pass inspection are presented, they will be mustered in at once and assigned to quarters."

Alexandria Gazette, May 14, 1863

Finally, Stanton agreed to move forward, but insisted that the entire regiment be raised and pass inspection (640 men) before being mustered in, a requirement never before imposed. In other words, there would be no appropriations to support the needs of the initial recruits. W.G. procured provisions and supplies out of his own pocket.[17]

Commissioner Dole successfully lobbied Stanton to remove the requirement that a full regiment of African American troops be raised before being mustered in. Instead, individual companies raised by W.G. and Turner would be mustered in as they were raised.

Secretary of War Edwin Stanton

As the formation of a regiment of blacks in the D. of C., is an undertaking which may succeed or may not, the Secretary of War has refused to authorize advances to the force that is forming, until the requisite number is obtained.

Alexandria Gazette May 16, 1863

> **The Colored Regiment in the District.**
> The Secretary of War to-day, on application of Commissioner Dole consented to receive the colored soldiers by companies instead of requiring the entire regiment to be raised before accepting it. The recruits are directed to meet at the Contraband Camp on Monday noon, when they will be mustered in and provided for.

Daily National Republican (Second Edition), May 16, 1863

> The Secretary of War has recognized the applications of Cols. Turner and Raymond to organize a colored regiment in Washington.— The Secretary of War will send mustering officers to muster them into the service to-day.

Alexandria Gazette, May 18, 1863

A passionate African American minister, Reverend Henry McNeal Turner, joined the effort to raise the initial troops.[18] His contribution was immediate. Recruiting posters and news stories got the word out. The Washington press corps enthusiastically covered the efforts.

Despite this progress, Washington's proximity to the South resulted in a divergent mix of viewpoints on Blacks enlisting in the Union Army. Many sympathizers for the survival of slavery roamed the city's streets. This made the recruitment of Blacks a perilous undertaking for both the recruiters and the recruits. But come forward, they did. Freedmen, former slaves, came forth to fight for their freedom in the most literal sense. Indeed, for the very liberty of an entire race. Among the multitude of perspectives that swirled during the Civil War, one White Union soldier stated, "They've as much right to fight for themselves as I have to fight for them."[19]

In his autobiography, W.G. related the account of an early recruiting meeting where an unidentified assailant shot through a window, the bullet just missing Raymond's head, having been deflected by the window sash.[20]

MEETING

For the Organization of a

COLORED REGIMENT

IN THE

District of Columbia.

The President has authorized Col. J. D. Turner, late Chaplain in the Army, and Lieut. Col. W. G. Raymond, late Chaplain in Trinity Hospital of this city, to raise a Regiment of Colored Troops in the District of Columbia.

A meeting will be held in Asbury Chapel, corner of 11th and K streets, on Monday evening next, May 4th, at 7½ o'clock, to organize, and make arrangements to visit the President and receive his orders.

All who desire to enlist in the 1st Regiment District Columbia Colored Volunteers, and thus demonstrate their manhood, are earnestly invited to be present, and hear, consult, and decide.

By order of—

J. D. TURNER,
W. G. RAYMOND.

Early Recruiting Poster

At a subsequent recruiting meeting, W.G. provided a status report on the recruitment effort. He then exhibited to great applause a regimental flag hand-made and donated by Julia Henderson, a local African American woman.[21] Her accompanying letter indicated that she hoped that the flag might be the first to enter the capital of the Confederacy, Richmond.[22]

In the same meeting, several advocates for the recruitment of Black Union soldiers spoke, reporting that African Americans stood ready to take up arms to secure the ascendency of their race as far away as Chicago.[23] There was even support from the British Navy. A Captain Thoret relayed that in his experience, African American soldiers and West Indian soldiers demonstrated success in the service of England and that their ". . . bayonets were never behind."[24]

Next to address the group was a Black man from North Carolina, Henry Johnson. He announced that he was enlisting as a soldier and fully expected to be killed.[25]

His wish was that his friends would bury him as they continued the fight.[26] He predicted that the returning African American soldiers would re-elect Abraham Lincoln.[27]

Driven by passionate purpose and despite all obstacles, they forged onward with tents, uniforms, arms, and provisions secured by Raymond and Turner.[28]

What would become the 1st United States Colored Infantry was born. First, however, and this is an important distinction, the unit would be named the 1st District of Columbia Colored Volunteers. Volunteers were essentially citizen militias. There was no assurance there would be any soldier pay for Black recruits, let alone on parity with White soldiers. Courageously fighting for their freedom was compensation enough for many.

Under the command of J.D. Turner and W.G. Raymond, hundreds of African American recruits, with more to come, were eager to fight for freedom and the Union. The recruits proudly marched the streets of Washington under threat of harm in mid-May 1863. They marched through taunts that even included those from members of their race.[29] During drills on Pennsylvania Avenue on the afternoon of May 21, a White man yelled ". . . you damned nigger!" to one of the soldiers. The African American soldier stood his ground and resolutely stated, ". . . I'm a soldier too, and there will be a fight if you insult me."[30]

The momentum and rapidity with which the federal African American troops were organized revealed the lack of a uniform and consistent framework encompassing federally raised Black troops and the growing number of state-level African American regiments.

Secretary Stanton sensed the operation rapidly assuming a life of its own. The United States War Department issued General Order Number

LOCAL AFFAIRS✓

ANOTHER WAR MEETING OF COLORED MEN.— Last night, according to appaintment, a meeting of colored citizens was convened at the Israel Bethel Church, near the Capitol, in aid of the regiment now forming. The large audience room was crowded.

The meeting was organized by the selection of Rev. H. M. Turner (colored) as chairman and Frank A. Taverns (colored) as secretary.

Lieut. Col. Raymond then gave a brief statement of the progress in the organization of the new regiment. It was expected that two companies would have been mustered in that day; but owing to delays in getting the men together in the forenoon, and the lateness of the hour before the order from the War Department could be obtained, the matter was deferred until the next morning. He also stated that the arduous duties which had devolved upon Col. Turner, and his active zeal in bringing matters to their present encouraging aspect, had worn upon his mind to such an extent as to cause his health to give way temporarily, and he was now quite ill, and unable to be present. He hoped the prayers of all the good among their people would ascend to the throne of grace for his recovery.

Col. R. then exhibited a beautiful silk flag—the stars and stripes—and stated that this had been presented to the regiment during the day by a patriotic colored lady, who, having been prospered herself in this world's goods, desired the prosperity and elevation of her race. The following letter, which accompanied the flag, was then read and greeted with tumultuous applause:

.WASHINGTON, May 18, 1863.

COL. RAYMOND: Please accept for your regiment this flag as a token of my good wishes, hoping that it may be the first to reach Richmond. Having been fortunate myself, I doubt not you will share the same luck with this banner.

I remain your sincere friend,

JULIA HENDERSON.

Daily National Republican (Second Edition), May 19, 1863

143 on May 22, 1863. This order established the Bureau of Colored Troops, charged with facilitating the recruitment of African American soldiers and other people of color not of African descent. These troops were folded into what became known as the United States Colored Troops or the U.S.C.T. The companies raised by W.G. Raymond, J.D. Turner and Henry McNeal Turner would become the 1st U.S.C.T.

President Lincoln showed keen interest in the success of these African American companies.[31] At the same time, the security of the soldiers and their officers was increasingly under siege. Southern sympathizers and other agitators disrupted the training exercises and potentially risked their deployment and lives.

Abraham Lincoln with Allan Pinkerton and Major General John A. McClernand

In early June of 1863, Lincoln set out to observe the initial troops of the 1st U.S.C.T only to discover that the War Department had, under secrecy even to himself, moved the troops to Analostan Island, also known as Mason's Island (later Theodore Roosevelt Island) in late May.[32] The island was in the Potomac River and provided a more secure location to complete the training for battle.

At this time, the command of the 1st U.S.C.T was abruptly transitioned to Col. William Birney.[33] Birney possessed more military and combat experience than J.D. Turner and W.G., but the full rationale for this change did not evade questioning among those close to the recruiting effort. In any event, J.D. Turner was experiencing debilitating health issues by that time, and W.G. needed to rebuild his finances after the bankrolling of the troops.

Indeed, W.G. had incurred great personal expense in the early raising of the 1st U.S.C.T. before the establishment of the Bureau of Colored Troops. He was able to rebuild some of his solvency through publishing and selling religious books that year.

Of profound significance for the country from the historic raising and mustering of the 1st U.S.C.T. was the commissioning of Reverend

Union Army guards the dock on Analostan Island

Henry McNeal Turner as the first African American Chaplain and officer in the Union Army. He had been a tireless recruiter for the troops and served the 1st U.S.C.T with distinction as they completed training and went into battle.

In response to proposals to test the battle worthiness of the Black troops against Native American populations perceived to be hostile, Chaplain Turner was fierce in his opposition to the idea:

". . . Like us, thou (Native Americans) hast been scattered and peeled, and you are fast marching down the road to extinction, and soon, I fear, will no longer be numbered among the races of the earth. Therefore, O Indian, how could I slay thee; how could I cut thy throat or put the dagger to thy heart?"

He opined that he believed the African American Union soldiers would hold the same perspective.[34]

The troops of the 1st U.S.C.T and subsequent regiments needed no such experimentation to demonstrate their battle readiness, courage, or

Reverend Henry McNeal Turner, Chaplain of the
1st U.S.C.T.

Fitzhugh Lee

Edward A. Wild

fierceness in fighting for freedom. The 1st U.S.C.T went on to engage in arguably the most successful battle waged by Black Union troops in the Civil War at the Battle of Wilson's Wharf on the James River in Virginia in May of 1864 (also known as the Battle of Fort Pocahontas).

Roughly 1,100 African American soldiers, most of them with the D.C.-raised 1st U.S.C.T Infantry, by then under the direct command of Brigadier General Edward Augustus Wild, guarded the depot installation at Wilson's Wharf.[35] Led by Confederate Major Fitzhugh Lee, nephew of General Robert E. Lee, up to 3,000 confederate soldiers attacked the installation.[36] After suffering heavy losses during the attack, Lee withdrew in the night hours and retreated in the direction of Richmond.

Against twenty Confederate soldiers killed and one hundred wounded, the African American troop loss was two killed and twenty-four wounded.[37] The 1st U.S.C.T and other units had victoriously secured the installation at Wilson's Wharf.

Sergeant George W. Hatton of the 1st U.S. Colored Infantry said of his regiment, ". . . the heroism displayed by the gallant [soldiers] of the 1st needs no comment, for they have won for themselves unfading laurels, to be stamped on the pages of history."[38] Another Union officer stated after the battle, "That the Black man will fight is an established fact."[39]

U.S.C.T. Troops in Battle

W.G. Raymond retained keen interest and pride in the 1st U.S.C.T. after they headed into battle, and he had departed for his missionary work in Kansas. (J.D. Turner had died during this period.[40]) The 1st U.S.C.T. had multiple engagements beyond Wilson's Wharf, including Chaffin's Farm, Fair Oaks, Petersburg, and the capture of Wilmington. It was mustered out of service in September of 1865.[41]

General Robert E. Lee surrendered in Virginia on April 9, 1865, which most historians consider as marking the war's conclusion, with the Union victorious.

U.S.C.T. Troops

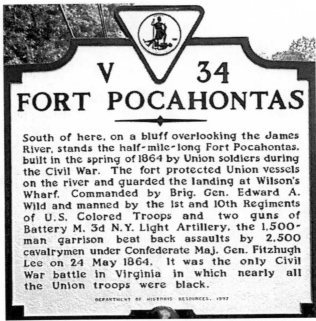

(Department of Historic Resources)

President Abraham Lincoln was assassinated less than one week later, on April 15, 1865, at Ford's Theatre in Washington. Sergeant John C. Brock, a Black soldier from the 43rd U.S.C.T., summed up the thoughts of many, so shaken by Lincoln's death, by writing: "Thank God! he was permitted to see the fruits of his toil . . . He still lives in the hearts of thousands, yea, millions of those whom he by his love of justice, liberty and his well-known belief in the right of man, redeemed from the curse of slavery . . ."[42]

Andrew Johnson, Lincoln's Vice President, assumed the presidency. Johnson was a Democrat and a Southerner. Among the reviewers and the President, W.G. attended the White House for the Grand Review of the Armies on May 23 and 24, 1865. On this occasion, W.G. related:

"I was highly honored a seat with the reviewers in front of the White House at the closing up of the war, when the victorious [Ulysses] Grant and [William T.] Sherman were marching in their last grand review before the President of the United States, with worn and riddled flags. As I looked upon this scene, that could but impress, those remaining boys in blue—that had left home, in manhood's strength and vigor—now returning, after weary marches—perchance, with sore and bare feet— while others had marched their last march—what a panorama presented itself to the mind's eye! What crushed longings and buried hopes—what homes that waited no coming greeting—but memories, like sorrowing mourners, were then, vainly seeking the last resting-places of those, who had borne away with them, so many of life's joys and dreams. Surely, what tongue can tell the miseries of war? None—none."[43]

There has been some controversy about the attendance, or lack thereof, of African American U.S.C.T regiments in the Grand Review. Most troops, however, were still located at various outposts of the War at that time. The 1st U.S.C.T was mustered out months later in September of that year.

The 1st U.S.C.T did receive their due recognition in October of 1865 on their return to Washington. Enthusiastic crowds gathered and cheered, and bands played as their steamer ship arrived.[44] Two days later, on October 10, the 1st U.S.C.T marched impressively and proudly to the White House, rifles at their shoulders, where President Andrew Johnson awaited.[45] President Johnson then reviewed and addressed the troops, much as he had done in the Grand Review months earlier. Importantly, Johnson enforced the principle of equality, referring to the African American soldiers as fellow countrymen. Johnson then expressed gratitude to the men for their service.[46] Owing perhaps to the rapidity of such momentous change, some of his comments were construed as condescending. Nothing, though, could quell the spirit and excitement of the day.

The 1st U.S.C.T. marched to Campbell Hospital following the President's remarks, where several dignitaries addressed the troops. A visibly proud W.G. Raymond made his way to the podium.[47]

With a voice described in the press as ". . . perfectly lion-like," and with a stature described as ". . . a most powerful frame . . . a formidable specimen of a Yankee soldier," W.G. Raymond expressed his pride in the soldiers[48] and gratitude to them. He related how he knew they would be successful. As had always been his hope, he conveyed that he harbored no doubt that these Black soldiers would go on to secure their full rights.[49]

Civil War Veterans of the U.S.C.T., Memorial Day Parade, New York City (Undated)

CHAPTER SIX

The Choppy Terrain Between Lincoln and Stanton

As W.G. and his colleagues discovered, the relationship between President Lincoln and Secretary Stanton would play a leading role in any initiative that required approving nods from both. This included the lightning rod effort to engage African Americans in the War, to fight for their freedom as Union soldiers.

Recall that Stanton was presented with Lincoln's orders to recognize J.D. Turner and W.G. Raymond as Colonel and Lt. Colonel, respectively, of a new federal regiment of African American volunteers from Washington D.C., and to do all he could to support them. Stanton scoffed and threw the order down on the table.[1] Through that reaction, much was revealed about the relationship between Lincoln and Stanton.

Stanton ran the War Department as a self-contained vessel, with him firmly in autonomous command. Lincoln was the Commander-in-Chief, but the President had to sleep on a cot in the telegraph office set up in the old library of the War Department Building to be able to monitor incoming telegraphs reporting on progress in the field of battle.[2]

Stanton reserved the right to choose the times and places for African American engagement in the War, and he would select who would lead these troops into battle. When the President stepped in to appoint the two commanding officers to launch the federal Black regiment, it was an affront. When Stanton imposed the unprecedented condition that W.G. and Turner must first raise 640 men before any of their companies were mustered into service, he was buying time and sending a signal to Lincoln.

Stanton envisioned the Bureau of Colored Troops reining all activities of Black Union Army soldiering, both at the state and federal levels, into one body, under his control. He appeared to want to press the reset button on the official start of Black Union Army engagement, at least at the federal level. Readers should draw their conclusions about how Stanton ranked these activities in terms of priority and relevance, but as a side note, the Bureau of Colored Troops was set up in the basement of the War Department.[3]

Recall also that the troops and companies raised by W.G. and Turner were hastily scurried out of Washington D.C. proper and onto a cloistered island in the Potomac, concurrent with General Order 143. This was under the auspices of providing better security for the troops as they trained. Tellingly, they were also moved away from Lincoln's daily line of sight and, at first, without his knowledge.

Despite Lincoln upsetting Stanton's sense of territory by appointing W.G. and Turner to lead the federal Black Union Army recruiting and soldiering effort and Stanton's well-documented early assessment of Lincoln as a bit of a rube, mutual respect grew over time. Much of this owed to Lincoln being able to overlook Stanton's characterizations of him as unsophisticated. Perhaps Lincoln even cleverly encouraged those perceptions to his advantage. In any event, they achieved an effective partnership in ultimately laying the groundwork to win the Civil War, with African American troops proving to be instrumental in that outcome.

Of what import, then, was Lincoln and Stanton's relationship to the life and efforts of W.G. Raymond? Despite being qualified, having been a Union infantry soldier and officer with the 86th New York Infantry Regiment, a chaplain, and being highly recommended as commanding officer by African American civic leaders in D.C. as well

as prominent U.S. senators, W.G. was stripped of his command immediately after the establishment of the Bureau of Colored Troops. The
War Department then hand-picked their leaders for the burgeoning
federal Black regiment.

The fallout of the slight Secretary Stanton seemingly felt when
W.G. was imposed upon him by President Lincoln would reemerge
many years later. W.G. would again pay a steep price for finding himself in the middle of this jousting of personalities.

With history-altering consequences.

CHAPTER SEVEN

Heading West after Washington

I n 1866 W.G. reached a pivotal moment in his life. His work tied to the Civil War was concluding. He had served as an enlisted man, a Chaplain, a change agent for the recruitment of African American soldiers, and as a War Department Detective after serving as a Baptist minister for more than twenty-five years.

During what may have been a chance meeting in the spring of 1866, he was encouraged by Dr. E.E.L. Taylor, Assistant Secretary of the Baptist Home Mission Society for the Indian Reservation, to consider a move to Kansas.[1]

What W.G. didn't know was that the second Baptist Mission in the newly formed state of Kansas was floundering. Because Dr. Taylor told him, he did know that the search had been on for the right person to take charge of the Indian school on the Pottawatomie Indian Reservation.

Dr. Taylor asked if W.G. "was at liberty" to consider the position.

W.G. replied, "I am for anything the Lord wants of me."

Soon thereafter, he packed up his family, closed his home and affairs in Washington, and headed west.[2]

"The following letters handed me just before we left Washington will show the appreciation of those with whom we had been associated, for four years, during the war," he notes of the below correspondence:

W.G. Raymond: Post Office, Washington, D.C., April 10, 1866
Rev. W.G. Raymond: My Dear Sir,

Permit me to join your many friends in this city in the expression of my good wishes for your future welfare and happiness and for your success in the new field of labor in which you are about to enter. Your patriotic course during the rebellion, the services you rendered our sick and wounded heroes, and your many noble acts which in command of the Provost Guard of this city, have endeared you to every loyal man in this District whose good will and friendship you will carry with you to your new and distant home. That you may find kind friends, those who will appreciate your motives and intentions, in the far-off West, is the ardent prayer of

Truly and sincerely your friend,
S.P. Bowen, Postmaster

Washington, D.C., April 10, 1866
Rev. W.G. Raymond: My Dear Friend and Brother,

Your mission field is changing. For some years you have been laboring in this vicinity and while endeavoring to do good to others you have allied yourself by warm friendships to many Christian hearts. In separating from you and bidding you farewell, I look with no small interest to that field which God has, I trust, selected for you. I hope you may be encouraged and blessed in your labors and even the unborn [Pottawatomie's] will in the future rise up to call you blessed. May God strengthen and bless you abundantly on earth, and give you a place in his kingdom at last.

Truly yours,
A. Chester

Patent Office Bureau Head, Washington, D.C., Headquarters Department of Washington 22nd Army Corps, April 10, 1886

The Rev. W.G. Raymond has been known to me for the last two years in connection with the services as Chaplain at one of our

hospitals, and his duties as a colporteur and friend of our soldiers,
I found him most faithful and devoted in his duties—active and
watchful for opportunities to do good to the sick and distressed. I have
a great regard for him as a sincere and devoted Christian and cordially
commend him to all with whom he is brought in contact in his new
field of labor.

    C.C. Augur, Major General

(Christopher Columbus Augur was born in New York in 1821. He and his family moved to Michigan, and in 1839 he entered West Point. C.C. Augur graduated in 1843 in the same class as future General of the Army and President Ulysses S. Grant.[3])

Did W.G. understand that Kansas was every bit the lightning rod that D.C. had been? He might have.

Kansas had only become a state in 1861. In the cross-currents of slavery and westward expansion, it had become what some would call the federal government's "dumping ground" for many displaced Native Americans. The Missouri Compromise of 1820 had been replaced by the Compromise of 1850, and the 1854 Kansas-Nebraska Act allowed slavery north of Missouri's southern border. Railroads were cutting paths westward, and that expansion was not without greed, deception, and an aggressive search for federal and other dollars to complete the tracks and stations that would soon connect throughout the United States.

"Bleeding Kansas," just a few years before his arrival (1854- 59), was a civil war between pro- and anti-slavery advocates; Kansas had been established on unsettled and conflicting soil. In 1856, John Brown had murdered five men in cold blood to send a message. He was a bold man whose beliefs centered on the notion that no man can be bound to another. He and his wife had twenty children and landed in Kansas to wage a bold and bloody counterstrike to slavery. He believed it was necessary to "strike terror in the hearts of the pro-slavery people." Setting out in the dark of night, Brown had entered the pro-slavery town of Pottawatomie Creek and stormed the houses of those he saw as enemies. He and his accomplices brutally killed five people.[4]

In response, John Brown's family home was burned to the ground.[5] John Brown's followers held that he had killed no one, but the thought prevailed that he decided which men would die and who would live. Now, as a fugitive, he headed north, where he was received as a hero by the Abolitionists. This action, and the action of those who responded to John Brown's attack, helped to turn Kansas into a bloody catastrophe.

Against this backdrop came W.G., eager to evangelize and spread the message of his Lord. Dr. Taylor had offered him 1,200 dollars for his year's work as superintendent of the Pottawatomie school on the Reservation. He had also indicated that Secretary James Harlan intended for the missionaries to be agents of the Reservation, and the salary for that office could mean an additional 2,000 dollars per year.[6]

Agents were authorized to serve by living among the Native Americans and guiding them "into acculturation of American society." Primary work objectives included preventing issues between the Native Americans and White settlers and overseeing the proper distribution of annuities granted by the state or federal government, usually extended between the agent and the Native American chief.

Federal monies followed the Pottawatomie Indian Treaties of 1846 and led to the establishment of the Second Baptist Pottawatomie Station in Kansas. The signees included leadership from the Native American tribes and "White" government and church leaders.[7] Notably, for the Pottawatomie, Jude Bourassa was a signee.[8] Jude was the son of Daniel Bourassa, who had been the first to sign muster rolls in the forced removal of the Native Americans to Kansas. Jude had received his education from Carey Mission in Niles, MI., and attended Hamilton Literary and Theological Institute, as had W.G, although there is no evidence that they were aware of one another or had studied there at the same time.

The Pottawatomie had endured and still were enduring turbulent times. During the 1830s, they had been forced by soldiers to begin a march to Kansas, leaving behind their more nomadic lives in and around the Great Lakes. This became known as the Pottawatomie "Trail of Death." Five percent of the tribe died on the trail. Survivors were then placed on a single reservation near Topeka.[9]

The school, which encouraged prayers, study, and classroom work, also taught girls how to cook and do laundry. In addition to instruction, the boys were engaged in learning blacksmithing and other trades. Their tribal essence was undeniably minimized as they gained Christian names and adopted a "White" manner of dress.[10]

The school ran from 1848 to 1861. Then, due to shortages of funds, staffing, and the outbreak of the Civil War, some shifts led to a closing. Five years later, a renewed effort was made with the school. The final phase of the long struggle by the Baptists to provide education to the Pottawatomie began in 1866. Luther R. Palmer, then agent to the Pottawatomie, described the new superintendent of the school, Rev. W.G. Raymond, as a man possessing "much energy."[11]

Indian Affairs Commissioner Dennis Nelson (D.N.) Cooley said that the school was being reopened "with flattering prospects in the old Baptist Mission building under the auspices of the Baptist Home Missionary Society."

W.G. wrote, "Arriving at the Reservation, I immediately commenced labor. The first effort I made was an application to the government for two thousand dollars to repair the building, and obtained it, and saw it well expended." Of W.G., D.N. Cooley wrote, "he has shown sufficient energy in making necessary preparation, repairing the mission buildings, &c., [and] now awaits the action of the board to enable him to open his school."[12]

Soon it was clear to W.G. that there would be no fulfillment of Dr. Taylor's promise to serve as agent, so he remained for just one year as the superintendent.[13]

"I left the Reservation moneyless but not friendless and launched out on to mostly missionary fields, moving my family to Auburn, Kansas, and agreeing to preach there one-half the time, the other half at Burlingame and other missionary points. My usual Sunday labors were three sermons and a ride of from three to ten miles, out and back.

CHAPTER EIGHT

Kansas, Regrets, Addiction, and Grasshoppers

W.G.'s time in Kansas gave root to regrets and the next few years plunged him into deep struggle and pain. His regrets weren't related to a change in his conviction that slavery was wrong—he remained confident of what was right and wrong on that score. He also remained confident in his work as a minister. Instead, his regrets were tied to the political issues he had become involved in as Kansas had emerged as a new state.

"Regarding my political life in Kansas, I refer to it reluctantly and with many regrets, although I believe I was on the right side of the political issue, which was liberty or slavery," he later recounted.

W.G. saw himself becoming "worldly" again, dabbling in railroad projects, holding railroad meetings, and using what he later felt was deception in bringing the projects before the people to "induce Eastern capitalists" to take on the responsibility of completing the railroad.

In W.G.'s own words: "There seemed to be, as I then thought, a necessity to engage in the politics of that new state. This I did faithfully and effectually, as many Senators, as well as Governors and other politicians, would testify. There is one consoling thought as I review this record, it is, that though I mingled intimately with infidels and scoffers of religion and many who were using bribes and deceiving and lying, I never accepted a bribe or handled money to bribe, nor willfully lied. I may have sometimes evaded, but I sought to out-general my antagonist and, in so doing so, formed alliances which I now consider unjustifiable for a Gospel minister. Not that I neglected the ordinary practical duties of my profession as a minister but felt in my devotional seasons when going before God, either in secret or in public, that I had not free access to the throne as I had had. Another thing I regret is my trafficking in blooded horses and fine stocks. Exhibiting them in fairs to compete for premiums, these premiums resulting in dissatisfaction."

The property gains he accumulated "chastened the Lord's hand upon me." Blow after blow struck him. First, his dear Lumanda became terribly ill. As his wife struggled, she wanted to return to Brookfield, Pennsylvania, to her family home. To fund the journey to take her and their children there, he put five of his prize horses on the auction block, along with his nearly completed large stock barn in Kansas.[1]

This he did, hoping the return to Brookfield would strengthen her. But Lumanda lived for only six weeks after her return to Brookfield. She died in the very room where her mother had passed not long before her. Lumanda's death was a crushing blow to W.G., and he remained in Brookfield for a year, becoming, in his words, "a grave worshipper." He hovered by her grave in despair.

By the year's end, his health had crumbled. He was plagued by several illnesses, each of which could claim him. He was in constant pain with ulcers, heart disease, liver, kidney, and bladder troubles. Even worse for him was the pain reliever to which he had become addicted: opium.

His good friend and physician Kent had advised that he take Bigelow's Purified Opium to relieve him from the colic he suffered.[2] Soon, he said, his habit of opium was "fixed." None of his health woes were cured, and he was now beholden to a drug that insidiously took over his body and life.

Dr. James Tyler Kent became famous as a high potency homeopath, with most homeopaths before him using only low potency remedies.[3] He taught Materia Medica at the Homoeopathic Medical College of St. Louis from 1881 to 1888, at the School of Homoeopathy, Philadelphia, from 1890 to 1899, at Hahnemann Medical College and Hospital, Chicago, from 1903 to 1909, and then at Hering Medical College Hospital.

He was the President and Trustee of Chicago Homoeopathic Hospital. In discussing details of W.G.'s serious health issues that led him to prescribe opium, Dr. Kent wrote:

"At that time, you were greatly prostrated, and fluctuation was found in your liver, which showed that there was an abscess. The prognosis became unfavorable. I remember that you vomited and purged a considerable quantity of bloody pus. This was the critical moment, and I remember you lost your head and passed into collapse. It was at this time that I administered to you a powerful narcotic (Opium), thinking that rest could only tide you over a crisis."[4]

By the mid-1800s, the first warnings about opium addiction were being sounded. But there was still a great deal of confusion. In 1833, Dr. C.L. Seeger from Northampton, Massachusetts, asked, "is opium an addiction and illness or a sign of a weak, immoral character?"[5]

Laudanum, a tincture of opium, was commonly used as a painkiller then—it was treated like Tylenol is today in its ease of availability and dispensing. There were no limits then on the drug's use, and there were

Dr. James Tyler Kent

no restrictions in the United States on who could purchase it.[6] The problems developed as people discovered they craved opium long after the headaches, body aches, and health challenges had passed.

The use of opium transformed the pain fields of the Civil War. The development of the hypodermic needle aided in its effective pain-relief delivery. Between 1872 and the creation of the Harrison Narcotic Act in 1914, opium had clearly gripped the souls of many and destroyed lives just as extensively as it reduced the intractable pain of wounded soldiers and others.

"I continued for ten years a hopeless invalid, suffering continually in my stomach, my only relief being by the use of the opium which I was seldom without. When suffering, I would have given a large sum rather than be without it," W.G. admitted.[7]

One fellow Civil War figure, who represented the Union, was held captive by the Confederates. When finally released, he was a fragment of his former self.[8] He had been deprived of food and left to rot in the heat and freeze in the cold. His stomach had hardened, and he was in constant pain. For the pain, his physician gave him "morphia."[9]

He later wrote of his intense battle with opium in *Opium Eating: An Autobiographical Sketch By An Habituate*, published in Philadelphia by Claxton, Remsen, and Haffelfinger, 1876. He wrote, "I found myself in the fangs of a monster more terrible than the Hydra of Lerna, and whose protean powers it is not man's to know til it is too late to escape." He described trying to quit and moving into an influx of melancholia and remorse, a "complete loss of command of oneself . . . stomach and bowels were unsettled, surging, and wishy-washy, constant flushes of heat and cold, a continual perspiration. My flesh seemed stretched tightly and my limbs pained me. My voice was hollow and weak." He felt "hopeless upon a dark and boundless sea, drifting further from land."[10]

W.G. knew this same demon, and he sought paths to escape its hold on him. He decided to return to Auburn, Kansas hoping that he could divert his mind from his diseases and restore his health. He promptly purchased a fine lineup of horses and kept his mind and body busy.

Whenever loneliness struck him, he would ride his horse four miles to his daughter Mary's beautiful farm so that he could "receive the sunshine of her smiles." But the smiles didn't last; Mary and her baby unexpectedly died and were laid to rest in a shared grave.[11]

W.G. was bitterly depressed and drifted from place to place in Kansas like a boundless tumbleweed, uncertain and restless.

There was no break for him. The next assault came in waves of millions. Grasshoppers—Rocky Mountain Locusts—filled the skies, blocking the sun and descending on crops, sheep, people's backs, and more.

It was the Grasshopper Plague of 1874, and soon everything that could be eaten and destroyed by them was. The drought conditions in Colorado, Montana, and Wyoming drove the locusts to seek and devour the prairies. The livestock that survived was scuttled off by the thousands to other states. People's lives and their livelihoods were driven into the ground.

Images from the time show exhausted folks raking the swarms into piles like fallen leaves, then burning the piles. Starvation and devastation went hand in hand as the creatures devoured food sources.

"The sound the locusts made was compared to the roaring of a huge waterfall. Not only were crops devoured in minutes, but so too was the wool from the bodies of live sheep and even, according to some reports, the clothes off people's backs. Trains couldn't move along the tracks because the insects made the rails too slippery."[12]

In *Bugged: How Insects Changed History*, Sarah Albee explains that since pioneers were left with nothing to eat, they were forced to boil the locusts to eat in soups.

"The air is literally alive with them," a *New York Times* correspondent wrote from Kansas. "They beat against the houses, swarm in at the windows, cover the passing trains. They work as if sent to destroy."[13]

The Cowley Historical Society Museum noted that: "In a single hour, fields of forty acres of corn have been entirely denuded of verdure and killed outright."[14]

One report released in 1874 suggested that just one family in ten had enough provisions to last through the coming winter.[15]

In late November 1874, Lt. Governor E.S. Stover held a relief meeting, and soon railroad companies were transporting aid to the destitute, bringing rice, beans, and pork from other areas.[16]

In this time of distress, W.G. received a lifeline: he was appointed by Kansas Governor Thomas A. Osborn to serve as a Solicitor for the Kansas Central Relief Committee. The appointment was effective on January 20, 1875. He was placed in charge of securing aid for the people of Shawnee County.[17]

> *Leavenworth, Kan., Jan. 27, 1875*
> *To Whom it concerns:*
> *The Bearer, Rev. W.G. Raymond, is a member in good standing in the Baptist Church in this city, and as such, is commended to the Christian sympathy and confidence of churches during his absence. I.S. Kalloch, Pastor*
> *Executive Department, State of Kansas, Topeka, Jan. 20, 1875*

> *To whom it may concern:*
> *In accordance with the foregoing request of the Kansas Central Relief Committee, W.G. Raymond, of Shawnee County, is hereby recommended as a proper person to receive contributions of aid for the needy people of his County. Thomas A. Osborn Governor*

It took some years, but then the Grasshopper Plague began to disappear just as mysteriously as it had started.

CHAPTER NINE

Becoming a Faith Healer: What it Meant to Him and to Others

W.G. was entering the last two decades of his productive life. He was fifty-six years old.

"The summer of 1875 was spent in Washington and Virginia, and my general health improved, but the local troubles were not removed . . . To my shame, as a Christian minister, I sought recreation and diversion in worldly amusements, such as dominoes, croquet, and checkers, even horse shows at fairs, and to please friends, theatres, and fishing parties. This, too, while under a sentence of death as regarded by the best physicians and several times during this period brought to death's door."

Still, he carried out what he felt was his most important work. "Some of the time, I would work notwithstanding all of the pain I had, until compelled to give up, for I was not only ambitious to live but to be active."

He noted that the sermons he delivered during this time were among his best. While in Falls Church, people from all denominations came to hear him preach as word of his sermons spread. "Let me say, however, souls were not saved by these efforts, and they were always followed by great physical and mental prostration and depression of spirits, and I would seek retirement in the woods and there plead with God to forgive and give me strength to break away from this bondage."

He left Virginia in the late fall of 1875 and remained through the winter with his brother, George C., in Clifton Springs, New York. Here he found himself in a better spiritual state and was engaged in revival services. He helped to organize and found the Baptist Church at Clifton Springs. There, he served as pastor until his ill health returned with a vengeance.

This time he had fully given up "worldly amusements" and sought comfort—but not yet health—in Christ.

Near Clifton Springs, he witnessed the healing of Martha Foster Inskip at Dr. Foster's Sanitarium in answer to the doctor's prayer of faith.[1]

"This made deep impression upon my mind—a medical man going ahead of ministers of the gospel in claiming the promises of God."

His declining health continued to command his thoughts. Finally, he decided to journey to Missouri to spend time with his brother, John C. Soon after, they took a family trip down the Mississippi River. It was as if Job had begun the trip: wind, rain, floods, and thunderstorms took control of their boat. On their return, "the water was so deceiving that it was taking the carriage right down the river, and only by a remarkable Providence did we all escape drowning." Their carriages and horses became mired in mud, and it took a full day to extricate them from the near catastrophe. Just after church the following day, a terrific cyclone came up. "The house was taken up as though it had been a feather and then let down without disturbing a dish on the table, which was set for supper."

W.G. spent the next few weeks baptizing and holding protracted revival meetings. But soon, his health was shattered, and his doctor urged him to rest or he would likely die.[2]

He returned to Kansas and helped, as much as he could, to farm at his daughter Ella and son-in-law's place in Burlingame. He remained there for nearly three years, enjoying renewed strength and time with his family.

Within the following months, his health again shifted, and it was as if he had no fight left within him. "I lost nearly all my spiritual enjoyment, and through not seeking [the] counsel of the Lord, but acting according to the wisdom of the world, I made the greatest mistake of my life—a mistake which brought bitter sorrow and mortification and brought me down into the very dust." He did not want to burden his family and instead left Kansas again.

After a few weeks of travel, he returned to the center of much of his early vibrancy and success, Washington, D.C. "I lost everything and was left in that great city where formerly I had enjoyed health, prosperity, popularity, and plenty of means, without a dollar, and physically and mentally a wreck."

His condition worsened, and he lost his ability to see his way out of this depression. "One day, I took my revolver, duly loaded, and started in the direction of the spot, where afterward God mercifully healed me, intending to take my own life. On my way, my children in the West came before me, also my ministerial life of forty-five years, and the blood of that would be upon my skirts, and the stain upon God's cause; so instead of going on, I turned aside into a little grove, and there fell down on my face and cried mightily to God to deliver me from the devil."

There was mercy in his weakest moment. He picked himself up and dusted off his clothes. He resolved to start again. Feeling too proud, under his present circumstances, to turn to former friends, he found a small room to rent on the third floor of a home on 14th Street. He lived simply, relying on bread and milk to sustain him. There were no creature comforts in his room.[3]

For five or six months, he lived a hermit-like existence. Finally, in a watershed moment, he "resolved to go down before God, by confession, prayer, and humiliation, to give up the world, the flesh, and the devil." He read only the Bible and a hymn book to strengthen his resolve. In the quiet of his days, he began to review his life.

"I reviewed my different pastorates, my relations to them, almost family by family, when I discovered mistakes, or errors of judgments, I treated them as such, but sins, I called them by their right name, and I implored God's forgiveness." In this time of intense review, God seemed far away from him. "His ear for mercy I could not gain."

He turned again to his Bible and found this passage: *If the salt has lost its savor, it is henceforth good for nothing.*[4] This passage, he believed, described him. He was obsessed not with the parts of his career and life that had been fruitful but instead clung to the unfavorable and questionable parts.

Long days and months passed, and still, he had no evidence that "the hand of the Lord was upon him." He felt no mercy. Then, on October 8, 1882, he held a pencil and stared at a blank sheet of paper. "I made with my pencil a figure zero. As my eye unconsciously fell upon it," I said, "Yes, Lord, nothing from nothing, leaves nothing, and I felt there was nothing left for me but death, and fell over on the bed in utter despair."

The sun rose the next day. He resolved to go into the woods of Rock Creek and to stay there until he should either die or feel a sense of renewal.[5] In a telling move, he left his key in the door so that if he did not survive, someone could enter the room. "I suppose I took an extra portion of opium, for, in the course of two or three hours, I reached the woods, just north of the city."

He felt compelled to go to various spots in the wooded spaces near a stream of water. Finally, he came to a spot in a grove of small trees, and he heard, "This is the place."

W.G. removed his coat, hat, and collar and laid his umbrella and cane on the ground. He could feel the warmth of the fall day on his grizzled face. He breathed in and could hear the birds as they sang their way from tree to tree.[6]

His mission had been to remove himself from the city so that he might better hear the voice of God. In this quiet space with just the sounds of nature, he heard nothing. He wept and waited. Then in his despair, he began to hear these words:

"You want to be forgiven of all of your sins and irregularities for over forty-five years, and you are not willing to forgive your own enemies."[7]

He was startled and looked to see who was voicing these words. He was alone in the grove. He tentatively said, "Lord, they haven't asked my forgiveness or shown any signs that they are sorry."

Stillness followed. The sun was shining above as it was now almost 11 a.m.[8]

"I stood up, facing the east. Looking to my right, I saw the cross and Jesus nailed to it, his face towards the east, and his left side towards

W.G. Raymond in the woods of Rock Creek

me. I saw a portion of his back, where it had been lacerated and was now bleeding. I saw the crown of thorns upon his head, pressed upon those temples, from which the blood was dropping, while those who had nailed him to the cross looked exhalant." Then he heard Jesus saying, "Father, forgive them for they know not what they do." And with that, the vision vanished.[9]

Then he heard the words, "Did Jesus wait until He saw signs of repentance, or until they asked His forgiveness?" The voice continued, "Read the 13th chapter of 1st Corinthians."

W.G. had Hamilton College President Kendrick's New Testament in his hand. He read the passage and said: "I saw more clearly than ever before that underlying the Christian religion was love."[10] He then began to hold up each of those he felt he needed to forgive, starting with Deacon Henry Fox of Kansas. He felt that he did not need to continue if he could not forgive this man.

He felt nothing. Then, he implored, "Lord, Jesus, help me, and I will forgive him." Until his dying day, W.G. prayed for Deacon Fox as he prayed for his children.[11]

One after another, in his mind, he pictured those he needed to forgive and could feel a power coming upon his head that seemed to pass right through him. "So thorough was I being dissected in every part of my body, painful while it was passing, so I thought it might be death."

Instead, his shoulders drew back, his chest filled out, and he felt health and new life fill his battered body. It was now high noon.[12] "I brought my right foot down and seemed to be standing on a rock. Thank God! I stand once more erect as a man. I am clean. I am healed!" All of his pain left him. He walked back and forth as if to test his new being. "I then leaped for joy and praised the Lord."[13]

Miraculously, in every moment after that until his death, he felt a full regeneration of his body. "The Lord removed from me all malice, all lust, and has thus far kept me by His power," he later wrote.

W.G. returned many times to this same spot in Rock Creek. He named it Beulah Land in consultation with God. "Beulah Land" ever after was also his most precious hymn:[14]

I've reached the land of corn and wine,
And all its riches freely mine;
Here shines undimmed on blissful day,
For all my night has passed away.

Chorus:
O Beulah land, sweet Beulah land,
As on the highest mount I stand,
I look away across the sea,
Where mansions are prepared for me,
And view the shining glory shore,
My heaven, my home for evermore.

The Savior comes and walks with me,
And sweet communion here have we:
He gently leads me with His hand,
For this is heaven's border land.

A sweet perfume upon the breeze
Is borne from ever vernal trees,
And flowers that never fading grow
Where streams of life forever flow.

The Zephyrs seem to float to me,
Sweet sounds of heaven's melody,
As angels with the white-robed throng,
Join in the sweet redemption song.

He would return there and remove his shoes to feel what he knew as Holy Ground under his feet. Sometimes he poured anointing oil on the nearby rock he named Rock of Ages.[15]

He felt that his remaining days were to be spent doing great work so that when Christ returned, W.G. would hear the welcome plaudit, "Well done thou good and faithful servant, enter thou into the joy of thy Lord."

He remained a changed and healed man. "In my Bible classes, I at once introduced into my teaching *healing for the body*, as well as for the soul, through faith in Christ . . . The first lady I met who believed this doctrine was Mrs. Dr. Duncan, a lady highly intellectual and of eminent piety who had been wonderfully raised up though not healed. She was the first I anointed for healing in the name of Lord Jesus. She was healed and arose from her bed and wanted to go and take charge of her mission.

"I shall never forget how I felt when she sent for me to come and anoint her with oil and pray for her, for I was even then ignorant of the teachings of the Word of God, as thousands in the ministry now are. I professed to be a Bible student. Yet my faith was simple and untrammeled by theories, such as divide and weaken the power of the faith people."[16]

For the first year following his healing, W.G. remained connected with the 14th Street Baptist Church and traveled to other Baptist Churches where he had been affiliated.[17]

Dr. Lodge, who had previously worked with W.G., called him to the Gay Street Baptist Church, Georgetown, D.C., as he was seeking someone to assist him in the pastorate. W.G. transferred his membership there from the 14th Street Church to work as Assistant Pastor, as a right hand in church work, Sabbath school, and Bible work.

In addition, W.G. worked throughout the city of Washington and the surrounding country to pray for and anoint the sick, according to James v:16–18.

One healing involved a woman who was a clerk in one of the government departments in Washington. She had been blind for more than a year and had to keep herself in a darkened room. "We anointed and prayed for her without any apparent immediate result. As we were rising from our knees, the gift of healing came upon me, and I said to her, 'My sister, you are healed now.'"[18] In that moment and after, she could see. She gave W.G. her glasses, which he kept as a memento of what the Lord had done.[19]

For three years, he worked within the Baptist Church and as a faith healer throughout the east coast. Then, in the spring of 1885, at the age of sixty-six, W.G. felt drawn out of denominational work altogether and into faith work exclusively. He left behind a salary, accepting any freewill offerings (no collections were ever taken).

W.G. Raymond near Beulah Land

W.G. Raymond at the "Rock of Ages"

He spent several months at intervals in Baltimore, Maryland, and stayed with two different families. He needed larger venues, and Mt. Pisgah Tabernacle was made available to him without cost by a Mrs. Stagmeyer. Here, throngs packed in every night. One man had been deaf for thirty years because of scarlet fever. "I placed my fingers in his ears, and in the name of the Father, Son, and Holy Ghost, commanded his ears to open. I asked, 'Can you hear me?'

'Yah,' he replied."[20]

Another woman spoke quietly to one of W.G.'s colleagues: "I have come one hundred and sixty miles to be cured of the consumption [tuberculosis]." Eight different physicians had treated her, and she was essentially given up to die. The last physician who had treated her had said that her lungs were full of "rotten matter." She was offered a short prayer, and hands were laid by Sister Robertson, one of W.G.'s colleagues, on her lungs. She was instantly healed and was found to be still healthy seven years later, on a follow-up visit.[21]

He traveled to the Eastern Shore, Maryland, Deals, New Market, Sharpstown, Vienna, Crotcher's Ferry, Portville Island, Laurel, and several other places in Delaware, before preparing for his next travels. During this time, a man named Howard, who claimed to be from Tennessee, arrived with his own agenda. He was, according to W.G., a man who had considerable oratorical abilities. But he was looking to prosper from what he saw as a fine opportunity. W.G. felt uncomfortable around the man: "there seemed to be a screen between him and me."[22] Mr. Howard raised some six or seven hundred dollars, purportedly for a new tent, then vanished into the night air.[23] When W.G. returned to Baltimore, he was told by Mrs. Stagmeyer that she would not give him the space any longer.

In time, he found a three-story brick house on N. Stricker Street, with a large basement and parlors in one of the best locations in Baltimore. It became the Beulah Land Faith Home.[24] He and his ministry were sustained by families who provided meals, furniture, provisions, and money to help defray the facility's costs. In time, the owner of the building, a physician, sold the structure.[25] W.G. and his colleagues were forced to seek a new home. Drawn east, they found a beautiful three-story brick building. The owner charged a low rent, and the staff worked to cut ice out of the alleyway and maintain the structure. This became the second Beulah Land.[26]

It was here that W.G.'s daughter, Mary Goldsmith, was healed. This was after a prominent physician had operated on her to remove cancer at the cost of 500 dollars.[27] She found renewed health and was "cleaned of soul and body," having passed close to death.

The crowning case of all W.G. had known was that of Minnie Addick, daughter of Dietrich John Addick, a ship carpenter who lived nearby on Canton Avenue. Four years earlier, she had been carried to the University Hospital. She was thirty years old and had spent thirteen years in bed. "Her diseases were complicated, but foremost of them were cancers in the stomach and breast." Cancer had been cut from her, and she was almost constantly under the influence of morphine by injection. The nails of her big toes had become infected, and she suffered amputations. She could not bear weight on her ankles.[28]

Her misguided Lutheran minister finally implored her to "be a good girl and die, as you can never get well. I have been up to the graveyard and have seen your lot, and it is a beautiful one. You have been sick long enough."[29]

Several of W.G.'s associates rendered care to her and prayed for her, but they gave up as Minnie refused to release the hold of her morphine. In days, W.G. and Sister Perry anointed her head and limbs with oil and, in the name of the Lord, united in prayer.

Minnie never again took to her bed as an invalid.[30] Two days after her initial healing, W.G. returned and saw her walking with a cane, bent over. He said, "Minnie, throw away that staff." After prayer, she straightened up and never again used it, although she was not as quick to overcome her morphine addiction.[31]

Eventually, Minnie came to W.G.'s healing center and reluctantly gave him her morphine and the needle. "I found she was covered with sores and her flesh rotten on the bones," W.G. noted.[32] His women assistants carefully bathed her in saltwater, and she found victory over the morphine "through Christ." She remained at the Beulah Land facility for ten weeks. She was later baptized in the river at Ferry Bar, Baltimore, and became a teacher of English in Norfolk, Virginia, then

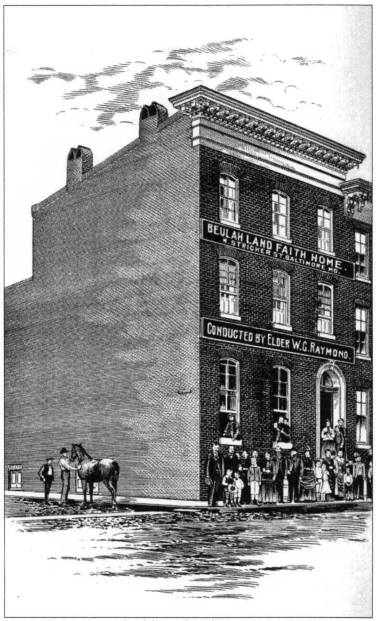

Beulah Land Faith Home

in Richmond, and finally in Scotland. Her experience was covered in the *Baltimore Herald*, the *Globe-Democrat* (St. Louis), the *Baltimore American*, the *Baltimore Sun*, and the *Vanguard*.[33]

Many faith-cure individuals were working throughout the country at the time. It had become, in fact, a movement, one which had both detractors and adherents. All its adherents held that salvation was tied to relieving the guilt of sin; some believed that sanctification eradicated sin, some that it suppressed it. What W.G. held was related to his personal experience in Rock Creek: "I have sought not only here in Lansingburgh, but wherever the Lord has led me to labor since He healed me, to lead the people to receive, and the saints 'to earnestly contend for the faith once delivered to the saints.'" (*Jude iii.*)[34]

He said that he baptized a candidate "neither into or out of any organization, but I baptize any who, like the Eunuch, apply for baptism on profession of faith in Christ and the Lord adds them to the Church. If they choose to work with any Christian organization, they are free to do so. We may be deceived and baptize one who has not been saved, but the Lord makes no mistakes.[35] The Lord leads me by the Holy Spirit to walk in daily service as Jesus walked; to labor and teach as I believe he labored and taught when on earth during his public ministry."

Briefly, W.G. summed up his work like this: "And Jesus went about . . . preaching the gospel of the kingdom and healing all manner of sickness and all manner of diseases."

W.G. also held to the concept of full immersion,[36] as in *John* iii:3: "Jesus answered and said unto him, 'Verily, verily, I say unto thee, except a man be born again, he cannot see the kingdom of God . . . Except a man be born of Water, and of the Spirit, he cannot enter into the kingdom of God.'" He believed that water and the Spirit were essential to the completion of salvation: "I believe that the Scriptures teach that when one believes in the Lord Jesus Christ and is immersed in the name of the Father, Son, and Holy Ghost, the Lord adds that one to the Church of God."[37]

For three years of Jesus' life, he ministered to the sick and afflicted. He was, as W.G. saw it, "the Savior of the body" and "he bears our sicknesses as truly as he bears our sins."

In December of 1887, at the age of sixty-eight, W.G. began to hold meetings in the Bethel ship, which had once been a California merchant vessel but had been purchased by several boatmen and fitted as a church.[38] "It is with heartfelt gratitude that I remember the generous freewill offering of the boatmen and the people of Jersey City," he recorded.

In August of 1890, H.B. (Harriet Frances Barnett) Hastings of Chelsea, Massachusetts, reached out by letter to Elder Raymond. Mrs. Hastings had heard reports of his labors and faithful teachings. At that time, W.G. was in Jamestown, New York, holding meetings that Harriet determined were worth traveling to witness firsthand: "I attended some of his meetings and saw an extraordinary case of healing, which caused my heart to rejoice more than ever, in the Great Physician of both body and soul."[39]

Harriet Hastings had been praying for someone to help in her Mission work and preach the full gospel to lost men and women. After meeting W.G., she invited him to come to visit her Mission.[40] W.G. traveled there and remained for eight months, bringing renewed blessings upon the work there. People came to the Mission from as far away as California. One gentleman, Nathaniel Hines, said that he wanted to be baptized; he was immersed by W.G. into the Mystic River, East Boston.[41]

THE BOATMAN'S BETHEL.
Where Meetings were held at Jersey City, during Winter of 1887-88.

The Boatman's Bethel

On July 4, 1891, W.G. reached his seventy-second birthday. His friends gathered for ice cream and brought the welcome gift of thirty-seven dollars to help with the publishing of his book, *Life Sketches and Faith Work*.[42]

"I believe that Sister Hastings," W.G. wrote, "in opening her house and entertaining the vast company in their large Library Room for months did much to advance the work of faith-healing and salvation." He also gave much credit to H.L. (Rev. Horace Lorenzo) Hastings. Mrs. Hastings would ask H.L. if Elder Raymond's often loud prayers above his study disturbed him. He replied, "Sometimes they divert my attention but let him pray; had I plenty of money, I would hire someone to pray all of the time in my house, for good work to prosper." Mr. Hastings was the writer of a book of hymns and was the editor of *The Christian*. He had the largest private library W.G. had ever seen.

One day, W.G. met a woman named Mrs. Clows of East Boston, just across the bridge from Chelsea, who permitted him to use her property fronting the Mystic River to perform baptisms, but warned, "I don't know how my husband will take it, as he is an infidel."[43] However, all was well after Mr. Clows himself said to his wife one day, "I believe I will go over and see that Doctor in Chelsea for they say he cures everything." He sought out W.G. and was "healed in five minutes, in the name of Jesus Christ." He "remained healed" and accommodated the healing immersion of countless others on his property.[44]

In the final eight years of his ministry, W.G. saved and healed, and baptized thousands. He stated that he ". . . cannot speak definitely of the large numbers that have been drawn nearer to Christ and are today leading a holier life."[45] He said, "I teach Faith healing, and witness the fruits of the Divine power . . . For there is nothing covered that shall not be revealed, neither hid, that shall not be known."

On September 29, 1893, four months before his death, W.G. wrote: "The number baptized in the Mystic River, East Boston, during my labors in Chelsea is up to date and the total within a few years, nearly six hundred."[46]

Towards the end of his life, he wrote: "The wisdom of this world made its painted window of the wise, the learned and the righteous, but the Savior of mankind became the architect of a new society. He rejected the noble and the wise and chose the common people, the very material that the wisdom of this world had condemned, and from the refuse of society, he has taken up the fallen sons of men and set them, like diamonds, to sparkle forever in the diadem of his glory."

Elder W.G. Raymond passed from this earth on January 15, 1893.

Baptism of Converts, "Faith Curists" at Greenville, Jersey City, NJ

CHAPTER TEN

Marriages and Children Known and Recently Uncovered

W.G. had married and lost two wives; both had passed away when their children were still young.

In the mid-1800s, men and women moved in rather separate spheres. The opportunities to become acquainted, mingle, or "court" were restricted. W.G. and Martha had a short courtship and soon felt that they should be "one flesh."[1] They were married at her stepfather Deacon Ferris' home in New York by Reverend Samuel Adsit.

W.G. described Martha as "standing high for her intellectual attainments, as also in the church for her piety." She was a schoolteacher until their marriage. Together, they had two children.

Daughter Mariamne (later known as Mary) was born in Livingston County, New York, where W.G. led the Baptist Church of Sparta. A wealthy family adopted her.

W.G. said the family had agreed to educate her "but failed to do as they promised and treated her so roughly that she was driven out into the world and floated down almost to death's door. God only knows what the dear child suffered. She has been gloriously saved and is doing wonderful work on the line of boats from New York to Buffalo. She has worked considerably with me in leading boatmen to Christ."

"Mary" became the wife of Captain Ira Goldsmith, who owned boats on the New York and Erie Canal and was "led to Christ and immersed in New York Bay."

W.G. next accepted a call to the church in Jasper, Steuben County, New York. Martha and W.G.'s eldest son, Edwin L., was born here. It was not long before W.G. moved to a missionary field farther south, to work in Troup's Creek, New York.

Martha died a "triumphant death" here. "My wife had been to me a helpmate indeed, and we had been in every sense of the word laborers together in the service of the Lord, but the great loss I sustained in her death was her gain."[2]

Martha's death occurred not long after Edwin L. was born. Martha had promised Hannah Simpson she could rear Edwin, as W.G. explained, "with the promise that they would adopt him as their child, which they failed to do, and as the relatives got the property, it demoralized my son until he nearly lost his soul."[3]

A short time later, W.G. moved his efforts to Brookfield, Tioga County, Pennsylvania, where, in one revival, he met a Squire Simmons' two daughters—"Lumanda, I baptized into the Baptist Church."

Two years passed, and he returned to Brookfield, where he found Lumanda once again.

"I felt it my duty to marry again, and the Lord showed me very clearly I was to marry Lumanda Simmons, the young lady I baptized during the great revival in Brookfield. She had been engaged in teaching several years and was a highly educated lady for that time. She proved a great help to me in my ministry."

Lumanda's father was a wealthy farmer and merchant. As a Universalist, he had fought against his daughter's baptism and was even more against her marriage to a poor Baptist minister. He thought his daughter would be "moved from place to place, never accumulating anything."[4]

They decided to marry without his blessing. W.G. went down to her boarding home before her school began in the morning. Together they rode his carriage to Elder Murdock's and were married in the Baptist Church. She returned to her school to carry on with her responsibilities.

When news reached the Squire, he was enraged.[5] Days passed, and the newly married couple was invited by her father to come home. Apparently, he became quite attached to W.G. "Up until the time of his death, I could not see that he thought any less of me than his other children," W.G. recalled.

After their wedding tour to Niagara Falls and Rochester by carriage, W.G. was called to the First Pulteney Baptist Church near Crooked Creek. There he purchased thirty acres of land. Their first daughter, Ella, was born there.

Within two years, as Squire Simmons had feared, they moved to Little Valley, Cattaraugus County, New York, a mission field. W.G. had no prospect of a salary. There he purchased nineteen acres of land. They lived there for four years. During this time, their daughter Mary Ann was born.

At the end of the four years, he traded his place in Little Valley for a timber lot of several hundred acres and a sawmill just above the city of Bradford, McKean County, Pennsylvania. He did this, in part, to be among pine timber for the benefit of his health. During this time, he also preached in and around Bradford. Their daughter Rosie was born here. Rosie and her husband, Eugene Roberts, of Auburn, Kansas, a Methodist minister, lived out their lives in Kansas on a farm near Auburn.

When W.G.'s health had improved, he exchanged his mill property for a house and lot in the village. "This property, Ex. Sheriff Hicks informed me several years ago was worth eighty thousand dollars . . . A clear title of the village property was conveyed to Lumanda Raymond, my wife, from (Daniel) Kingsbury, who owned an immense tract of land."[6]

W.G. and Lumanda were called to Brookfield as her mother was gravely ill. While there, he received a call to the church in Harrison Valley, just above Westfield, Tioga County, Pennsylvania, and to the church in Brookfield. In Harrison Valley, he assisted in building "a very commodious and beautiful church, free of debt . . . Remember, these were mission fields, hence my moving about. I might have had more lucrative positions and longer pastorates with more opportunity for mental culture. I chose such fields because other competent ministers were unwilling to take them on account of the small income."

In Harrison Valley, Lumanda and W.G.'s son Willie G. was born but died in infancy. Their second son, Willie the 2nd, was born in Painted Post, New York, and died in Washington, D.C., when he was just three years old. "He was a remarkably smart child, and his death produced great sadness in the family." Willie was buried in the Congressional Grounds in Washington.[7]

During their time on the Pottawatomie Reservation in Kansas in 1866, Lumanda gave birth to a third boy named Willie. One Pottawatomie Chief offered to adopt him and let him live with W.G.[8] Instead, he lived with his sisters until he came of age. "It has been a great regret of the family that he did not continue his studies at Ottawa University, a Baptist institution in Kansas, until he graduated," W.G. recounted. W.G. was also left to search for evidence that Willie had been saved—"Let all the saints pray for his salvation," he wrote.

In summary, with his first wife, Martha, W.G. fathered two children: Mariamne and Edwin. With his second wife, Lumanda, W.G. fathered six; Ella, Mary Ann, Rosie, and three sons; William G., who died at three-years-of age, an infant named Willie, who also passed away, and William A., who was born on the Pottawatomie Reservation and survived into adulthood.

He was without a wife after Lumanda's death in 1872. But was he without a wife for long? Civil War Pension records indicate, and Census Records confirm, that he married a third time and fathered two more children: a boy and a girl. His third wife was Lucy Kitchingman, the widow of William Kitchingman, who had died in November of 1876 in Kansas.[9] Lucy was eighteen years younger than Kitchingman; they had had five children: three boys and two girls. After Kitchingman's death, she was faced with rearing their children, who were all under seventeen, alone.

How W.G. and Lucy became acquainted is not clear. W.G. lived with his daughter Ella Porter and her husband at their Auburn, Kansas farm. Lucy Kitchingman and her five children lived in Douglas County, Kansas, nearly thirty-five miles from there.

There is evidence of a marriage license filing between W.G. Raymond and Lucy Kitchingman in 1878. In 1880, the U.S. Census showed W.G. living with his wife, Lucy, twenty-one years his junior, in Bradford, McKean County, Pennsylvania. Two of her children from her marriage to Mr. Kitchingman, Nettie, age fourteen, and George,

4. MARY ANN RAYMOND.
3. ROSIE RAYMOND.   2. ELLA RAYMOND.
1. MRS. LUMANDA RAYMOND.
6. MARIAMNE RAYMOND.   5. WILLIE A. RAYMOND.
7. EDWIN L. RYAMOND.

The Raymond Family

age four, were listed. Also listed was Lucy and W.G.'s son, Frank Gould Raymond, age nine months. Within the year, Lucy and W.G. had a second child, a daughter, Lucy Jane.

From 1880 through to his death on January 15, 1893, no current research finds they lived together. In his book, *Life Sketches and Faith Work*, written from his notes over many decades, no mention is made of Lucy or their two children.

The Committee on War Claims Rewrites History

In 1882, nineteen years after those wild and momentous weeks before the establishment of the Bureau of Colored Troops, the U.S. House of Representatives again reviewed W.G.'s claim for reimbursement of expenses incurred raising those very first African American troops. Funds out of his own pocket, requested in an amount accounted for with preciseness so befitting the man—$843.[1]

The following exhibit is the official judgment of W.G.'s claim for $843, buried in a volume of House Committee on War Claims records. The conclusion was that W.G., a man who nearly took a bullet in the head for his efforts, had virtually nothing to do with raising the first federal Black recruits, those brave men who stepped forward on the rowdy streets of D.C. The Committee proclaimed that there was no record of W.G. ever having any role or participation in the U.S.C.T. W.G. Raymond's rightful claim for reimbursement was lumped together with what the Committee deemed as "bills without merit."

This judgment, of course, defies numerous Washington, D.C., newspaper accounts of W.G.'s troop recruiting activities, rigorous historical treatments, and even Lincoln's Presidential Papers, as shown throughout this text.

The sacrifices made by W.G. Raymond, J.D. Turner and Reverend Henry McNeal Turner in the early weeks of May 1863, were swept

W. G. RAYMOND.

APRIL 7, 1882.—Laid on the table and ordered to be printed.

Mr. HOLMAN, from the Committee on War Claims, submitted the following

REPORT:

[To accompany bill H. R. 2348.]

The Committee on War Claims, to whom was referred the bill (H. R. 2348) for the relief of W. G. Raymond, report as follows:

This bill authorizes the Secretary of the Treasury to pay W. G. Raymond an indefinite sum of money for money alleged to have been expended by him in recruiting for the First Regiment Colored Volunteers of the District of Columbia.

A communication from the Adjutant-General, establishes the fact that the claimant never performed any service in connection with the organization of said regiment. The Adjutant-General, in his communication under date of March 29, 1882, says:

Upon careful examination no record is found on the files of this office that W. G. Raymond was authorized to recruit for the First United States Colored Troops (First District of Columbia Colored Volunteers), or that he did recruit for that regiment, or perform any service whatever in connection with its organization. Upon examination of the rolls not one man of the regiment is found to have been enrolled by W. G. Raymond. In June, 1863, Mr. Raymond applied for appointment as an officer of United States colored troops, but was rejected by the board convened to examine candidates for such appointments. In October, 1863, he applied for payment of the sum of $843, which he claims was due him "for salary as lieutenant-colonel First District of Columbia Colored Volunteers, for two months, and recruiting expenses." This claim was rejected (and the papers returned to the claimant) on the ground that there being no evidence of service, either as a recruiting agent or as an officer of the regiment, payment could not legally be made.

It is one of the many claims that may be aptly termed bills "without merit," and the committee report adversely, and recommend the bill do lie upon the table.

WAR DEPARTMENT,
Washington City, March 31, 1882.

SIR: I have the honor to acknowledge the receipt of your letter of the 21st of January last, referring House bill 2348, to compensate W. G. Raymond for his expenses and money expended in recruiting the First United States Colored Troops (First District of Columbia Volunteers), and in compliance with your request for information in the case, to inclose a report from the Adjutant-General of the 29th instant, which contains, it is believed, such data as the committee desires to obtain.

Very respectfully, your obedient servant,

ROBERT T. LINCOLN,
Secretary of War.

Hon. L. C. HOUK,
Chairman Committee on War Claims, House of Representatives.

Committee on War Claims Record

under a bureaucratic rug. Indeed, it is seemingly the contention of the official record that W.G. Raymond, who had been appointed Chaplain of United States Hospital at Washington D.C., was willing to risk his reputation and integrity to defraud the government of $843. A scheme that would have required collaboration with the Washington press corps, future historians, and Lincoln himself.

As documented throughout this text, W.G. was a meticulous man with a moral fabric woven of iron. He was promoted to 1st Lieutenant only three days after enlisting in the 86th New York Infantry.[2] He harbored a reverence for justice and righteousness to such a degree that he would become noted in a Pulitzer Prize-winning account of Washington, D.C. history.[3] President Lincoln thought enough of W.G. to promote and appoint him Chaplain of the Washington hospitals. He held numerous endorsements from U.S. Senators and prominent civil leaders.

His passionate support for the rights of freed slaves and all African Americans to fight for their very freedom is above reproach. He put his own money, his very life, where his heart and mouth were. He was compelled to raise the first federal African American regiment in the Union Army against ridiculous odds and risk of death.

Beyond the abundant evidence supporting W.G.'s contributions, this purging of the official recognition of his activities in raising the 1st U.S.C.T. is perplexing and bold, given the overwhelming support both W.G. and J.D. Turner had from the African American community in Washington. Dozens of influential African Americans signed letters sent to Secretary of War Edwin Stanton in April 1863, endorsing W.G. and Turner as the initial officers of the first federal Black regiment. See exhibits of letters from the Lincoln Presidential Papers at the Library of Congress.

In addition to these letters of support, W.G. was honored with placement on the Registry of Notable People at the African American Civil War Museum for his 1st U.S.C.T. contributions. Yet an examination of official records would lead one to believe that W.G. had nothing to do with the raising of 1st U.S.C.T.

Letter of Support for W.G. From African American Civic Leaders (page 1)

Letter of Support for W.G. From African American Civic Leaders (page 2)

LIBRARY OF CONGRESS

Abraham Lincoln papers

From James M. Edmunds to Abraham Lincoln [With Endorsement by Lincoln][1], April 29, 1863

1 Both Turner and Raymond were clergymen. For their project to recruit a black regiment, they also had the endorsement of the Washington, D. C. Union League. See Raymond to Lincoln, April 25, 1863, and *Collected Works*, VI, 212.

General Land Office

April 29th 1863

Sir.

It has come to my knowledge that Mr. James D. Turner, & Wm G. Raymond desire authority to raise and Command as Col & Lieut Col, a Regiment of Colored Soldiers, to be raised in this District and within 30 days.

I have no hesitation in Saying that these are just such men as Should be entrusted with this duty, and if the responsibility was on my hands I would have them at the work without delay

Very Respectfully

Your Obt Svt

J M Edmunds

[Endorsed on Envelope by Lincoln:]

Colored Regiments in D. C — 1863

Abraham Lincoln papers http://www.loc.gov/resource/mal.2320800

Letter of Support for W.G. from J.M. Edmunds

There is a record of a subsequent bill, in January of 1883, H.R. 7262 for the 47th Congress, 2nd Session, again seeking to reimburse W.G. for his expenses to raise the 1st U.S.C.T.[4] The outcome of any vote or resolution to the bill has not been found.

That W.G. Raymond's and J.D. Turner's contributions to the raising the 1st federal African American Union soldiers have been erased from War Department records is not in question. The government has chosen to record the commencement of all federal Black Union Army activities as May 22, 1863, with the establishment of the Bureau of Colored Troops.

The question is, why?

Why officially disassociate from those remarkable and courageous early Black recruits who were willing to sign up to train without uniforms, without provisions, until paid for out of W.G.'s own pockets? Willing to march in front of often hostile and dangerous crowds, enduring unspeakable taunts?

Perhaps this early effort got ahead of the government's ability to provide for properly and protect the Black recruits and their officers, and even to pay them properly as soldiers. The War Department was caught flat-footed at a momentous and foundational moment in U.S. history. The hasty establishment of the Bureau of Colored Troops provided the opportunity to tidy up the embarrassing loose ends and rein these activities into a proper bureaucracy. Put them in the shade. Take control and ownership of the unfolding history, moving forward in a better light. The message to Lincoln and to history was that Stanton was in full control from the start. Which from then forward, would be May 22, 1863.

W.G. Raymond was laid to rest and honored with burial in Arlington National Cemetery. His headstone lists his service as 1st Lieutenant, his final rank with the 86th of New York. His appointment from President Lincoln to Lieutenant Colonel of the 1st District of Columbia Colored Volunteers, before the establishment of the Bureau of Colored Troops, is not engraved.

Does it matter? Do the few weeks of recruiting African American federal troops prior to the establishment of the Bureau of Colored Troops mean anything? Is it sufficient to simply state that federal African American troop activity commenced with the establishment of the Bureau as declared by the War Department and be done with it?

Respectfully, we assert that those few weeks do matter. The activities of W.G. Raymond and J.D. Turner were directly authorized by President Lincoln. Imagine the courage it took to step forward as a Black man in Civil War Washington. To sign up to fight, without the formal structure and assurances of the Bureau of Colored Troops yet in

W.G.Raymond's Headstone at Arlington National
Cemetery

place, with no pay, let alone uniforms and basic provisions. To openly
march and drill on the streets of D.C., amidst many Confederate sympathizers and skeptical northerners, many of whom would be fighting
alongside. To step forth to say, "Yes, I will fight!"

Or consider the prospect of being the Lincoln-appointed commanding officers of these regiments, only to lack the clear and forceful
support and sponsorship of the War Department. To struggle to provide basic provisions for your recruits from your own meager resources.
To go on to suggest that those few perilous weeks never happened,
as egregiously occurred years later in the War Claims Committee of
the House of Representatives, is a profound injustice. Those who were
there, assuming those risks, deserve better. As does history itself.

We believe we have researched and provided an uncommonly
fair and annotated assessment of the life, activities, and motivations

of W.G. Raymond. We only hope that his memory receives a degree of acknowledgment for his courageous and generous contribution to securing the right of African Americans to fight for their freedom. And for attending to the spiritual needs of scores.

Acknowledgment overdue.

Endnotes

CHAPTER TWO

1. Raymond, William Gould, *Life Sketches and Faith Work,* 5.
2. Ibid., 7.
3. Ibid., 8.
4. Ibid.
5. Ibid., 12.
6. Ibid.
7. Ibid., 21.
8. Ibid., 16.
9. Ibid.
10. Ibid.
11. Ibid.
12. Ibid., 18.
13. Ibid., 19.
14. Cathcart, William, *The Baptist Encyclopedia,* 264.
15. Raymond, 21.
16. Ibid.
17. Ibid., 22.
18. Ibid.
19. Ibid.
20. Ibid., 23.
21. Ibid., 24.

CHAPTER THREE

1. Raymond, William Gould, *Life Sketches and Faith Work,* 32.
2. Ibid., 33.
3. Ibid.

4. Ibid., 34.
5. Ibid.
6. Ibid.
7. Ibid.

CHAPTER FOUR

1. Raymond, William Gould, *Life Sketches and Faith Work,* 36.
2. Ibid.
3. *The National Republican,* Washington, D.C., August 14, 1862.
4. Ibid.
5. Raymond, 42.
6. Ibid.
7. Leech, Margaret (1941). *Reveille in Washington 1860–1865,* 327.
8. Raymond, 48.
9. Ibid., 49.
10. *The Washington Times,* "Conflicting Portraits of a Rebel," December 7, 2002.
11. Ibid.
12. Ibid.
13. Ibid.
14. Raymond, 45.
15. www.senate.gov United States Senate, Wilson, Henry, 18th Vice President (1873–1875) (Accessed 2021).
16. Raymond, 45.
17. Ibid., 46.
18. www.wikipedia.org Raymond, William Gould (Accessed 2021).

CHAPTER FIVE

1. Furgurson, Ernest B. (2004). *Freedom Rising,* 233.
2. Winkle, Kenneth J. (2013). *Lincoln's Citadel,* 339.
3. Glatthaar, Joseph T. (1990; 2000). *Forged in Battle,* 121–122.
4. Cornish, Dudley Taylor (1956; 1987). *The Sable Arm,* 96.
5. www.nps.gov *The Civil War's Black Soldiers: Contributions to Union Victory* (Accessed 2021).
6. Selected Antislavery Statements by Chautauqua County Baptists and some of their Neighboring Baptists: Excerpts from Annual

Meetings 1838 through 1862. By Douglas H. Shepard and Wendy Straight, 2015 1842: At the Fourth Session of the Harmony Baptist Association.

7. Gibbs, C.R. (2002). *Black, Copper, & Bright: The District of Columbia's Black Civil War Regiment,* 25–27.

8. Ibid., 26.

9. Ibid., 25.

10. Winkle, 330.

11. Gibbs, 25–26.

12. Ibid., 25.

13. Raymond, William Gould, *Life Sketches and Faith Work,* 51.

14. Ibid.

15. Winkle, 330.

16. Raymond, 52.

17. Raymond, 52.

18. Ibid., 331

19. Cornish, 93.

20. Raymond, 51.

21. Gibbs, 35.

22. Ibid.

23. Ibid.

24. Ibid., 36.

25. Ibid.

26. Ibid.

27. Ibid.

28. Raymond, 52.

29. Gibbs, 34–35.

30. Ibid., 39–40.

31. Winkle, 331.

32. Ibid., 333–334.

33. Ibid., 334.

34. Cole, Jean Lee (2013). *Freedom's Witness: The Civil War Correspondence of Henry McNeal Turner,* 99

35. Gourdin, John R. (2014). *117 Facts Everyone Should Know About African Americans in the Civil War,* 128.

36. Ibid.
37. Ibid.
38. Gibbs, 197.
39. Trudeau, Noah Andre (1998), *Like Men of War*, 219.
40. Gibbs, 171.
41. Gourdin, 114.
42. Trudeau, 434.
43. Raymond, 41.
44. Gibbs, 164.
45. Ibid., 166.
46. Ibid., 167.
47. Ibid., 171.
48. Ibid.
49. Ibid.

CHAPTER SIX

1. Raymond, William Gould, *Life Sketches and Faith Work*, 52.
2. www.history.com Christopher Klein, July 9, 2020 (Accessed 2021)
3. Winkle, Kenneth J. (2013). *Lincoln's Citadel*, 333.

CHAPTER SEVEN

1. Raymond, William Gould, *Life Sketches and Faith Work*, 56.
2. Ibid.
3. www.wikipedia.org Christopher C. Augur (Accessed 2021).
4. www.civilwaronthewesternborder.org Rein, Christopher, *Pottawatomie Massacre: Civil War on the Western Border: The Missouri-Kansas Conflict, 1854–1865.* The Kansas City Library (Accessed 2021).
5. www.ushistory.org *The Pottawatomi Creek Massacre*, U.S. History Online Text Book (Accessed 2021).
6. Raymond, 56.
7. www.kshs.org *The Pottawatomi Baptist Manual Labor Training School*, Barr, Thomas P., Winter 1977 (Vol 43, No. 4), 377 (Accessed 2021).
8. Ibid.

9. www.potawatomi.org (Accessed 2021).

10. *The Topeka Capital-Journal C-J Extra:* "Pottawatomi Mission: Part of Kansas' Early History," Cole, Jessica, March 13, 2018.

11. www.kshs.org Barr, 377.

12. Ibid., 425, Footnote 114.

13. Raymond, 56.

CHAPTER EIGHT

1. Raymond, William Gould, *Life Sketches and Faith Work,* 72

2. Ibid.

3. www.wholehealthnow.com *Biography Database: 150 Homeopaths Past and Present,* Kent, James Tyler, Dr. (Accessed 2021).

4. Raymond, 282.

5. www.wbur.org/commonhealth Bebinger, Martha, *As the Opium Trade Boomed in the 1800s, Boston Doctors Raised Addiction Concerns,* August 1, 2017 (Accessed 2021).

6. *Smithsonian Magazine,* "Inside the Story of America's 19th Century Opiate Addition," Trickey, Eric, January 4, 2018.

7. Raymond, 73.

8. Polizzi, Harry (2013) *Opium Eating: An Autobiographical Sketch by an Habituate,* Maine Book Barn Publishing, Originally Published (1876) Philadelphia: Claxton, Remsen, and Haffelfinger, Chapter 6.

9. Ibid.

10. Ibid., Chapter 7.

11. Raymond, 73.

12. Albee, Sarah (2014). *Bugged: How Insects Changed History,* New York: Bloomsbury Publishing, 107.

13. www.legendsofkansascity.com/grasshopper-plague *Legends of Kansas History, Tales and Destinations in the Land of Ahs* (Accessed 2021).

14. www.cchsm.com Cowley County Historical Society Museum, Topeka, Kansas. *Daily Commonwealth,* August 8, 1874 (Accessed 2021).

15. www.historynet.com *1874: The Year of the Locust,* Lyons, Chuck (Accessed 2021).

16. www.legendsofkansascity.com/grasshopper-plague *Legends of Kansas History.*

17. Raymond, 74.

CHAPTER NINE

1. Raymond, William Gould, *Life Sketches and Faith Work,* 80.
2. Ibid., 78.
3. Ibid., 82.
4. Ibid.
5. Ibid., 83.
6. Ibid.
7. Ibid.
8. Ibid.
9. Ibid., 84.
10. Ibid.
11. Ibid.
12. Ibid.
13. Ibid.
14. Ibid., 85.
15. Ibid.
16. Ibid., 87.
17. Ibid., 87–88.
18. Ibid., 89.
19. Ibid.
20. Ibid., 91.
21. Ibid., 92.
22. Ibid.
23. Ibid., 93.
24. Ibid., 102.
25. Ibid., 103.
26. Ibid., 105.
27. Ibid.
28. Ibid., 106.
29. Ibid.
30. Ibid., 107.
31. Ibid.
32. Ibid.
33. Ibid.
34. Ibid., 113.
35. Ibid., 115.

36. Ibid.
37. Ibid., 116.
38. Ibid., 158–159.
39. Ibid., 188.
40. Ibid., 188–189.
41. Ibid.
42. Ibid., 207.
43. Ibid., 209.
44. Ibid.
45. Ibid., 248.
46. Ibid., 289.

CHAPTER TEN

1. Raymond, William Gould, *Life Sketches and Faith Work,* 24.
2. Ibid., 25.
3. Ibid., 289.
4. Ibid., 26.
5. Ibid.
6. Ibid., 28.
7. Ibid., 287.
8. Ibid., 288.
9. Probate Record: Ketchingman, William: November 13, 1876: Record of Wills, Volumes 1–2, 1873–1901.

CHAPTER ELEVEN

1. *Committee on War Claims Record,* April 7, 1882
2. www.civilwargazette.faithsite.com May 17, 2007 (Accessed 2021)
3. Leech, Margaret (1941). *Reveille in Washington 1860–1865,* 327.
4. Raymond, William Gould, *Life Sketches and Faith Work,* 52.

Selected Bibliography

Albee, Sarah (2014). *Bugged: How Insects Changed History,* New York: Bloomsbury Publishing.

Brewster, Todd (2014). *Lincoln's Gamble,* New York: Scribner.

Cathcart, William (1881). *The Baptist Encyclopedia,* Philadelphia: Louis H. Everts.

Cole, Jean Lee (2013). *Freedom's Witness: The Civil War Correspondence of Henry McNeal Turner,* West Virginia: West Virginia University Press.

Cornish, Dudley Taylor (1956;1987). *The Sable Arm,* Lawrence, Kansas: University Press of Kansas.

Dameron, J. David (2017). *African Americans in the Civil War,* U.S.: Southeast Research Publishing, LLC.

Furgurson, Ernest B. (2004). *Freedom Rising,* New York: Alfred A. Knopf.

Gibbs, C.R. (2002). *Black, Copper, & Bright: The District of Columbia's Black Civil War Regiment,* Silver Spring, Maryland: Three Dimensional Publishing.

Glatthaar, Joseph T. (1990; 2000). *Forged in Battle,* Baton Rouge, Louisiana: Louisiana State University Press.

Gourdin, John R. (2014). *117 Facts Everyone Should Know About African Americans in the Civil War,* Virginia: Schroeder Publications.

Knapp, Jacob (1868). *Autobiography of Jacob Knapp,* New York: Sheldon and Company. Republished by Wentworth Press.

Laidlaw, Zoe and Lester, Alan (2015). *Indigenous Communities and Settler Colonialism,* New York: Palgrave Macmillan.

Leech, Margaret (1941). *Reveille in Washington 1860–1865,* New York: The New York Review of Books (NYRB).

Lowry, M.D., Thomas P. (1997). *The Civil War Bawdy Houses of Washington, D.C.* Virginia: Sergeant Kirkland's Museum and Historical Society, Inc.

Polizzi, Harry (2013) *Opium Eating: An Autobiographical Sketch by an Habituate,* Maine Book Barn Publishing, Originally Published (1876) Philadelphia: Claxton, Remsen, and Haffelfinger.

Raymond, William Gould (1891). *Life Sketches and Faith Work,* Boston, Washington Press: George E. Crosby & Co. Printers. Library of Congress, 1892. (Reproduced as public domain)

Smith, John David. (2013). *Lincoln and the U.S. Colored Troops,* Carbondale, Ill.: Southern Illinois University Press. (Kindle Edition)

The Abraham Lincoln Association (1953). *The Collected Works of Abraham Lincoln, Volume VI,* CT: The Easton Press with permission of Rutgers University Press.

Trudeau, Noah Andre (1998). *Like Men of War: Black Troops in the Civil War 1862–1865,* New York: Little, Brown and Company.

White, Jr., Ronald C. (2009). *A. Lincoln,* New York: Random House.

Winkle, Kenneth J. (2013). *Lincoln's Citadel,* New York: W.W. Norton & Company.

PERIODICALS

The Washington Times, "Conflicting Portraits of a Rebel," December 7, 2002

The Topeka Capital-Journal C-J Extra: "Pottawatomi Mission: Part of Kansas' Early History," Cole, Jessica, March 13, 2018

Smithsonian Magazine, "Inside the Story of America's 19th Century Opiate Addition," Trickey, Eric, January 4, 2018

The National Republican, Washington, D.C., August 14, 1862

WEBSITES

www.senate.gov United States Senate, Wilson, Henry, 18th Vice President (1873–1875) (Accessed 2021) www.wikipedia.org Raymond, William Gould (Accessed 2021)

www.civilwaronthewesternborder.org Rein, Christopher, *Pottawatomie Massacre: Civil War on the Western Border: The Missouri-Kansas Conflict, 1854–1865.* The Kansas City Library (Accessed 2021)

www.wikipedia.org Christopher C. Augur (Accessed 2021)

www.ushistory.org *The Pottawatomi Creek Massacre,* U.S. History Online Text Book (Accessed 2021)

www.kshs.org *The Pottawatomi Baptist Manual Labor Training School,* Barr, Thomas P., Winter 1977 (Vol 43, No. 4) (Accessed 2021)

www.potawatomi.org (Accessed 2021)

www.historynet.com *1874: The Year of the Locust,* Lyons, Chuck (Accessed 2021)

www.wholehealthnow.com *Biography Database: 150 Homeopaths Past and Present,* Kent, James Tyler, Dr. (Accessed 2021)

www.wbur.org/commonhealth Bebinger, Martha, *As the Opium Trade Boomed in the 1800s, Boston Doctors Raised Addiction Concerns,* August 1, 2017 (Accessed 2021)

www.legendsofkansascity.com/grasshopper-plague *Legends of Kansas History, Tales and Destinations in the Land of Ahs* (Accessed 2021)

www.cchsm.com Cowley County Historical Society Museum, Topeka, Kansas. *Daily Commonwealth,* August 8, 1874 (Accessed 2021)

www.nps.gov *The Civil War's Black Soldiers: Contributions to Union Victory* (Accessed 2021)

www.civilwargazette.faithsite.com_*William Gould Raymond,* May 17, 2007 (Accessed 2021)

www.history.com *How Abraham Lincoln Used the Telegraph to Help Win the Civil War,* Christopher Klein, July 9, 2020 (Accessed 2021)

All photographs, illustrations and exhibits are in the public domain.

Index

About the Authors

Donna Burtch is an American writer and poet. Her early life involved moves throughout and across the United States. Books and reading smoothed the transitions.

She settled in central Ohio in 1976, where she graduated from Ohio Wesleyan University and completed graduate studies at The Methodist Theological School in Ohio. Donna worked for several decades in marketing and fund-raising for firms, not-for-profits, and universities.

In 2011 she committed to National Novel Writing Month (NaNoWriMo). Ten years later she self-published her work as a biography of her late father's life, *In the Key of Sea: The Life & Times of William A. Burtch*. She and her family live in Columbus, Ohio.

William Burtch is a writer of fiction and essays. He was a finalist for the *American Fiction Short Story Award*, appearing in *American Fiction Volume 17* (New Rivers Press). William's creative work spans magazine, journal and anthology publications, including *Great Lakes Review, Ruminate, Northwest Indiana Literary Journal, BULL, Schuylkill Valley Literary Journal* and others.

Following a childhood that spanned the Allegheny Mountains of northwestern Pennsylvania to the sprawl of Los Angeles County, he has lived in central Ohio since his teen years. After graduate school at Miami University of Ohio, he worked many years in the investment business before he began writing. His work often gravitates toward the experiences and struggles of the rural characters he grew up around, as well as themes of survival in a culture of addiction.

His cherished late wife, Kari, lived courageously with ovarian cancer for three and a half years. She was selfless and inspirational and taught him about living. She gifted him with perspective.

William lives in Columbus, Ohio.

Made in USA - Crawfordsville, IN
79039_9781620069080
05.06.2022 2038